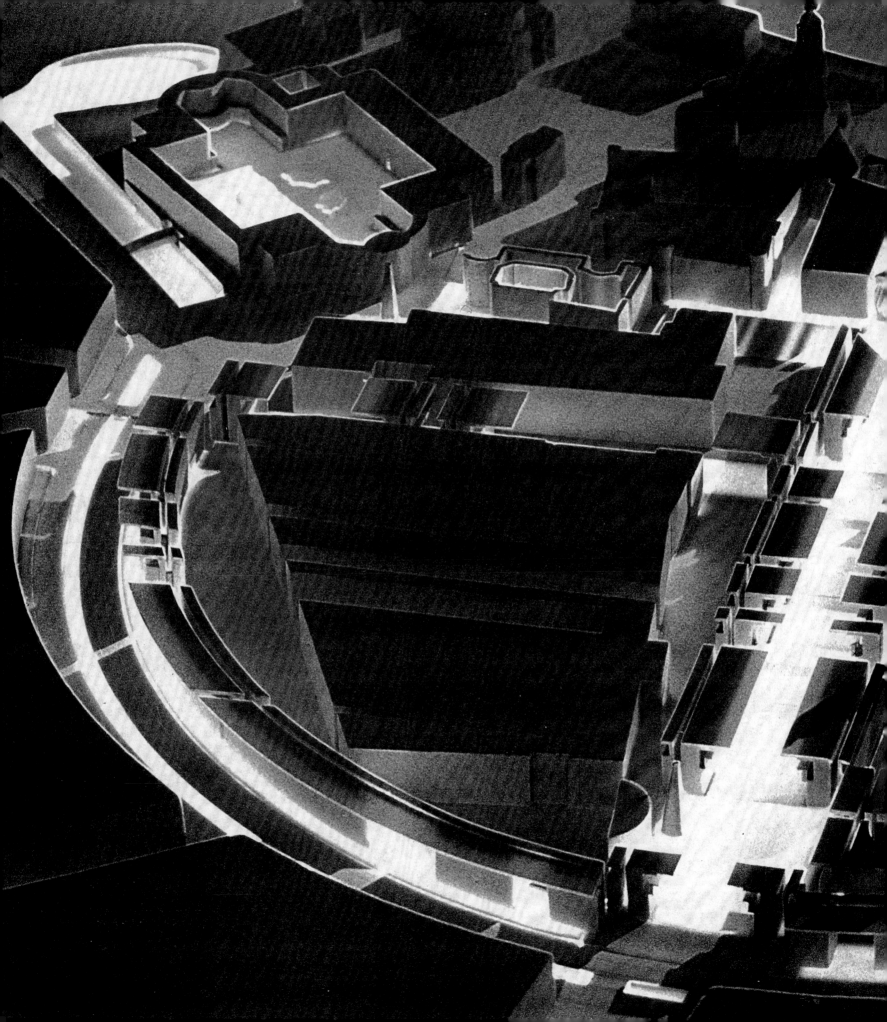

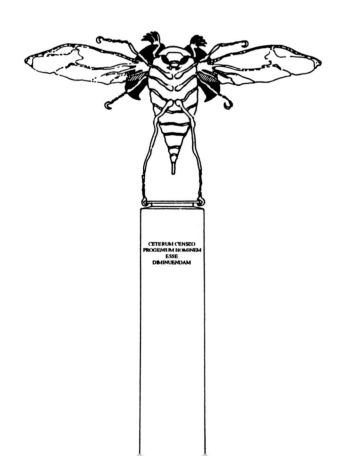

Axel Schultes

18

Edition Axel Menges

Axel Schultes

in Bangert Jansen Scholz Schultes

Projekte / Projects 1985–1991

Vorwort / Introduction   Wolfgang Pehnt

Herausgeber / Editor   Charlotte Frank

Ernst & Sohn

© 1992 Axel Schultes

Vertrieb/distributed by: Ernst & Sohn Verlag für Architektur und
technische Wissenschaften, Berlin

ISBN: 3-433-02328-X

Alle Rechte vorbehalten, besonders die der Übersetzung in andere Sprachen. Kein Teil des Buches darf ohne schriftliche Genehmigung in irgendeiner Form reproduziert werden.

All rights reserved, especially those of translation into other languages. No part of this book may be reproduced in any form without written permission.

Reproduktionen/Reproduction: Repro GmbH Fellbach,
Fellbach-Schmiden
Gigant Foto, Berlin

Druck und Bindearbeiten/Printing and Bindung: Grafos SA, Barcelona

Konzeption und Gestaltung/Conception and design: Charlotte Frank

Übersetzung/Translation: Michael Robinson

Die Texte, mit Ausnahme der Einleitung, sind von Axel Schultes.
The text, with exeption of the introduction, is by Axel Schultes.

Inhalt

Einleitung von Wolfgang Pehnt	25
Potsdamer Bahnhof, Berlin, 1991	37
Potsdamer Platz, Berlin, 1991	39
Gewerbepark Gladbeck-Brauck, 1991	47
Deutsche Bank Unter den Linden, Berlin 1991	51
Bürozentrum Hemmerichsweg, Frankfurt, 1991	53
Berlin Friedrichstadt, 1991	57
Altmarkt, Dresden, 1991	65
Piazzale Roma, Venedig, 1990	71
Rathauserweiterung Witten, 1990	75
Dachaufbau Lützowplatz 7, Berlin, 1990	79
Expo '92 Sevilla, 1990	81
Haus der Geschichte, Stuttgart, 1990	87
Wohnen an der Hasenheide, Berlin, 1989	93
Büropark am Welfenplatz, Hannover, 1989	97
Haus am Michel, Hamburg, 1989	99
Tokyo International Forum, 1989	103
Internationaler Seegerichtshof, Hamburg, 1989	111
Bibliotheca Alexandrina, 1989	117
Berlin Museum, 1989	125
Dachaufbau Lützowplatz 7, Berlin, 1989	133
Familiengericht, Berlin, 1989	135
Intercity-Hotel, Berlin, 1988	139
Parlamentsvorzone Bonn, 1988	141
Deutsches Rheuma-Forschungszentrum, Berlin, 1988	143
Verwaltungsgebäude der Schering AG, Berlin, 1988	147
Deutsches Historisches Museum, Berlin, 1988	155
Rathauserweiterung Witten, 1987	163
Lützowplatz 5, Berlin, 1987	167
Museum für Völkerkunde, Frankfurt, 1986	169
Kunst- und Ausstellungshalle Bonn, 1986	173
Städtisches Kunstmuseum Bonn, 1985	181
Hängepartie	189
Vita	191
Mitarbeiter	192

Contents

Introduction by Wolfgang Pehnt	25
Potsdamer Bahnhof, Berlin, 1991	37
Potsdamer Platz, Berlin, 1991	39
Gladbeck-Brauck business park, 1991	47
Deutsche Bank Unter den Linden, Berlin 1991	51
Hemmerichsweg office centre, Frankfurt, 1991	53
Berlin Friedrichstadt, 1991	57
Altmarkt, Dresden, 1991	65
Piazzale Roma, Venice, 1990	71
Extension to Witten Town Hall, 1990	75
New roof at 7 Lützowplatz, Berlin, 1990	79
Expo '92 Sevilla, 1990	81
Haus der Geschichte, Stuttgart, 1990	87
Living in Hasenheide, Berlin, 1989	93
Welfenplatz office park, Hanover, 1989	97
Haus am Michel, Hamburg, 1989	99
Tokyo International Forum, 1989	103
International Tribunal for the Law of the Sea, Hamburg, 1989	111
Bibliotheca Alexandrina, 1989	117
Berlin Museum, 1989	125
New roof at 7 Lützowplatz, Berlin, 1989	133
Family Court, Berlin, 1989	135
Intercity-Hotel, Berlin, 1988	139
Zone outside the parliament building in Bonn, 1988	141
German Institute for Rheumatism Research, Berlin, 1988	143
Schering AG offices, Berlin, 1988	147
Deutsches Historisches Museum, Berlin, 1988	155
Rathauserweiterung Witten, 1987	163
5 Lützowplatz, Berlin, 1987	167
Museum für Völkerkunde, Frankfurt, 1986	169
Kunst- und Ausstellungshalle Bonn, 1986	173
Städtisches Kunstmuseum Bonn, 1985	181
Game adjourned	189
Vita	191
Collaboraters	192

Vorbemerkung

Nur Narr, nur Künstler – nur die eigene Sprache sprechen, den eigenen Ausdruck finden wollen in unserer schönen Raum-Kunst – dieser notwendigerweise egozentrischen Ambition entsprach eine in den letzten Jahren immer offener gestaltete Partnerschaft mit Dietrich Bangert, Bernd Jansen und Stefan Scholz, die mit dem Jahreswechsel 1991/92 ein Ende gefunden hat.

Eine konzeptionelle Mitarbeit an den hier veröffentlichten Projekten ist vor der jeweiligen Entwurfserläuterung benannt, eine umfassende Zusammenstellung der beteiligten Architekten ist am Ende des Buches zu finden.

Ohne die Entschossenheit von Charlotte Frank und ohne ihr Geschick wäre die Herausgabe dieses Bandes ein frommer Wunsch geblieben. Ihr Augenmerk galt dabei weniger einer antiquarischen Dokumentation der Arbeiten – sie sind weder vollständig noch systematisch wiedergegeben – es galt eher dem Herausarbeiten einer entwurflichen Quintessenz.
a.s.

Preliminary remark

Just a fool, just an artist – just wanting to speak my own language, to express myself in my own way, within this wonderous art of space – an increasingly loosening partnership with Dietrich Bangert, Bernd Jansen and Stefan Scholz, which came to an end at the beginning of 1992, was correspondend to this necessarily egocentric ambition.

Collaboration on concepts for the projects published here, is acknowledged in each case before the commentary; a full list of the architects involved can be found at the end of the book.

Without the skill and determination of Charlotte Frank this volume would have remained a pious hope. She was concerned, not so much to ensure antiquarian documentation of the works – which are not presented completely or systematically – but much more with distilling the quintessence of design.
a.s.

Tuffsteinbruch in Les Baux

the tuff quarry in Les Baux

Die Welt von innen

Vermutungen zum Werk von Axel Schultes

The world from inside

Conjectures about the work of Axel Schultes

Die Phantasie hat eine bevorzugte Richtung: nach oben. Gebilde der Vorstellungskraft werden gern als luftig beschrieben. Allegorien der Phantasie kommen leichtfüssig daher. Pegasus hat Flügel. Bei Schiller trägt der 'fortgeschrittene Mensch' auf erhobenen Schwingen die Kunst mit sich empor. Euphorion, im Faust, die Verkörperung der Poesie, wirft sich in die Lüfte: 'Immer höher muss ich steigen/Immer weiter muss ich schauen.' Architekten haben sich am Höhenrausch fleissig beteiligt. Die babylonischen Türme aller Zeiten, die Milehigh-Nadeln Frank Lloyd Wrights, die luftigen Stadtgerüste der Metabolisten und Archigram-Leute greifen in die Wolken, die Träumer noch darüber hinaus: zu Mond und Sternen, Planeten und Milchstrassen.

Diejenigen, die in die umgekehrte Richtung träumen, sind in der Minderheit. Aber es gibt sie, die der Phantasie der Luftschiffer den Hang zum Subterranen, der Gralsburg den Hörselberg entgegensetzen. Höhlenforscher, Schatzsucher, Archäologen besitzen etwas von dieser nach unten gerichteten Imagination. Verborgene Minerale, vergessene Kostbarkeiten, die der Erde zu entreissenden Spuren vergangenen Lebens lösen ihre Faszination aus. Für Leute ihrer Art wird, wie für Alice in Wonderland, der Kaninchenbau zum Eingang in die Wunderwelt, zu Königssaal und Tränensee. Sie lassen sich, wie bei Jules Verne, von keiner geologischen Schulmeinung davon abhalten, den Einstieg ins Erdinnere zu suchen. Bei Paul Scheerbart, dem Inspirator vieler Architekten, geht es komfortabler zu. Sein Münchhausen benutzt den Luxuszug, um kolossale Bergwerke zu bewundern, groteske Felslandschaften, einen Grottentempel (in dem es Kaffee und Kuchen gibt), eine Tiefsee unter der Erde.

In diesem Band, der die Entwürfe des Berliner Architekten Axel Schultes aus den letzten Jahren vereint, verdanken die meisten Projekte ihren Reichtum einer Kombination beider Denk- und Blickrichtungen. Dagegen finden sich, beispielsweise, keine Hochhäuser, auch dort nicht, wo Schultes' Kollegen bei derselben Aufgabe, am selben Bauplatz sich der Lust des himmelstürmenden Bauens hingeben. Beim Hochhaus sind aber die Möglichkeiten beschränkt, Innenraum anders als in der Wiederkehr identischer Geschosse zu entwickeln. Wo Schultes Türme verwendet, lässt er sie aus einer Grube, einer Versenkung, einer Umwallung aufsteigen, so dass sie durch die Tiefe an der Höhe gehindert sind. Manchmal liegen nur 5 Meter 30 oder 7 Meter 50 unter der Erdbodenkante, manchmal auch 16 Meter 50 wie beim Ausstellungsbereich des Stuttgarter Daimler-Benz-Projekts, auf jeden Fall aber genug, um die Vorstellung des tief unten Gegründeten und Festgemachten zu erzeugen. Was unterhalb der Horizontlinie vorgesehen ist, sind nicht nur Sockel und Keller, sondern *Adventures Underground,* wie Lewis Carrolls Alice-Buch zuerst hiess.

In den späten sechziger und siebziger Jahren, in denen die Architektur bei den Leuten rapide an Kredit verlor, mag es ein Impuls skrupulöser Architekten gewesen sein, ihre Produkte so weit wie möglich den Augen der Mitmenschen zu entziehen. Was im Boden versteckt war, riskierte nicht, den Unmut der Zeitgenossen zu wecken. In der empfindlichen Nachbarschaft historischer Bauten hegt auch Axel Schultes solche Gedanken. Aber zu lustvoll inszeniert er seine subterrestrischen Bauwerke,

Imagination has a preferred direction: upwards. Products of the imagination are often described as airy. Allegories of the imagination trip on light feet. Pegasus has wings. Schiller's 'progressive man' carries art upwards on soaring pinions. Euphorion, in 'Faust', the embodiment of poetry, bounds into the air: 'Ever higher must I climb/Ever further must I see.' Architects have always revelled in the intoxication of height. Towers of Babylon throughout the ages, Frank Lloyd Wright's Milehigh Needles, airy cities designed by Metabolists and Archigram people reach for the clouds; dreamers reach even further: to the moon and to the stars, the planets and the milky way.

Those whose dreams go in the other direction are in a minority. But there are people who present an inclination towards the subterranean as an alternative to airborne fantasy, caverns measureless to man, and not the mountains of the moon. Potholers, treasure hunters, archaeologists, all their imaginations reach downwards. Hidden minerals, things precious and forgotten, traces of a world gone by that can be wrested from the earth, all have their fascination. For people like this, as for Alice in Wonderland, a rabbit hole is an entrance to a world of miracles: a royal chamber and a pool of tears. Like Jules Verne, they do not allow the geology of scientists to put them off a journey to the centre of the earth. Things are rather more comfortable in the works of Paul Scheerbart, who inspired a number of architects. His Münchhausen takes a luxury train to admire unfathomable mines, grotesque rocky landscapes, a temple grotto (with coffee and cakes) and a deep underground lake.

This volume brings together the last seven years of Berlin architect Axel Schultes' work. Most of the projects owe their richness to a combination of looking into both heights and depths. But there are no highrise buildings, not even where Schultes' colleagues succumbed to heaven-storming pleasures for the same project and on the same site. High-rise buildings offer only limited possibilities of developing interior space, other than in repeating identical storeys. When Schultes uses towers he lets them climb out of a pit, a hollow, a rampart, so depth checks back their height. Sometimes only 5 metres 30 or 7 metres 50 are below ground level, but sometimes as much as 16 metres 50, as in the exhibition area for the Stuttgart Daimler-Benz project, but always enough to give the idea of something founded and secured in depth. Not only bases and cellars are planned below the line of the horizon, but *Adventures Underground,* as Lewis Carroll's Alice book was first called.

In the late sixties and seventies, when architecture rapidly fell from public grace, scrupulous architects may well have been inclined to take their products as far away as possible from the eyes of their fellow men. Things hidden in the ground did not run the risk of falling foul of contemporaries. Even Axel Schultes harbours such thoughts in sensitive proximity to historical buildings. But he stages his subterranean work with such relish that it is impossible to mistrust his motives for long. Plazas are cut open so that we can look and move downwards, revealing wondrous caskets where prodigies are kept: a Petrified Forest or a Tent of Stone, an island in a groundwater lake or even Yggdrasil, the World Ash Tree. Light trickles down over artificial terraces, conical envelopes, stumpy pyramids, terraced cascades. Light fittings hang from ceilings

die grüne Wand in Schönbrunn

the green wall in Schönbrunn

als dass an dieses Motiv lange zu glauben wäre. Plaza-Ausschnitte mit Blick und Zugang nach unten offenbaren Wunderboxen, in denen Mirabilien aufbewahrt sind, ein Steinerner Wald oder ein Steinernes Zelt, Inseln in Grundwasserseen oder gar die Weltesche Yggdrasil. Licht rieselt nach unten, über künstliche Terrassen, Kegelmäntel, Pyramidenstümpfe, Treppenkaskaden. Beleuchtungskörper hängen wie Stalaktiten von den Decken. Öffnen sich Schächte und Höfe, so wird der Blick von der Sohle des Bauwerks aus steil hinauf gerissen. Es sind die Orte, wo Höhen- und Tiefenmenschen in gleicher Weise befriedigt werden. Nie ist der Tageshimmel so blau, sind die Sterne so gross, als wenn man ihrer aus den Schlünden und Kerkern der Erde ansichtig wird. Hans Guckindieluft und der Mann, der in die Grube fährt, sind zwei Personen in einer.

Schultes ist mit diesem Konzept auf ein aktuelles Thema gestossen. Denn in den grossen Städten wandern immer mehr Funktionen unbefriedigt in den Untergrund: die Rohr-, Kanal- und Leitungssysteme der Infrastruktur ohnehin, der ruhende und der rollende Verkehr auf Schiene und Strasse, die Verknüpfungsstellen von Trassen und Benutzern mit Foyers, Service-Einrichtungen und Einkaufspassagen. Früher waren Bahnhöfe wie Stadttore entworfen, heute, in den dicht überbauten Cityanlagen, sind die Gruben im Untergrund. Die Tiefbau-Spezialisten werden diesen modernen Hades nicht erlösen könnne. Wenn sie nicht durch Gestalt befreit werden, bleiben diese städtischen Souterrains eine vernachlässigte Unterwelt, bedrohlich wie die dunklen und unzugänglichen Bereiche des Unterbewussten, die den psychisch Kranken heimsuchen.

Unter allen denkbaren Bauaufgaben hat der Museumsbau diesen Architekten besonders beschäftigt. Der Anteil dieser Gattung an den Projekten und realisierten Bauten ist überproportional auch dann, wenn man einrechnet, dass Ausstellungs- und Museumsbauten im letzten Jahrzehnt einen höheren Prozentsatz des öffentlichen Bauvolumens ausmachten als in vielen Jahren zuvor. Schultes hat immer wieder die Gelegenheiten genutzt, die sich bei den einschlägigen Wettbewerben in der Bundesrepublik boten: bei den Häusern der Geschichte in Berlin und Stuttgart, bei der Weltausstellung von Sevilla, den Bonner Museen an der Friedrich-Ebert-Allee, dem Frankfurter Völkerkundemuseum. Für ihn scheint ein Zusammenhang zwischen dem Thema Museum oder Ausstellungsbau zu bestehen und dem 'Tiefgang', den er liebt. Das Museum bewahrt, was aus den Abgründen der Vergangenheit auf uns gekommen ist, aus der – wie Thomas Mann es genannt hat – 'Brunnentiefe der Zeiten', 'wo der Mythos zu Haus ist und die Urnormen, Urformen des Lebens gründet'. Die Entwürfe des Architekten antworten mit der Tiefe des Raumes auf die Tiefe der Zeit; sie nötigen den Gast zur vorübergehenden 'Fahrt in die Grube'. Der Weg nach unten, durch die geologischen Schichten, ist ein Weg zurück in die Geschichte. Die Geschichte wird wörtlich genommen als das Geschichtete. Sogar in diesem Buch geht Schultes so vor. Er gräbt sich von der Oberfläche des Jahres 1991 zurück in die eigene Biographie.

Bei einer beträchtlichen Zahl von Entwürfen bewirkt Schultes den Anschein des Aushöhlens, Einkerbens und Durchschluchtens auch bei vollem Tageslicht. Das Internationale Forum in Tokio, der Seegerichtshof

like stalactites. When shafts and courtyards open, the eye is carried steeply upwards from the floor of the building. These are places in which lovers of heights and lovers of depths can be equally content. The daytime sky is never so blue, the stars never so big, as when we see them from the gorges and cellars of the earth. Johnny Head-in-Air and the Man who Went to the Deep, Dark Cave are one and the same person.

Schultes turns to a present day topic with his concept. Servicing in mayor cities is increasingly moving underground in a very unsatisfactory pattern: severage, pipelines, and cabeling anyway; traffic on rails and roads, moving or non-moving; interjunctions of the user with the services such as terminals, entrance halls, and shoping areas. Railway stations were once built as gateways to the city. In overdeveloped areas they are now pits in the dirt. Civil servant engeneers are incapable of converting this Hades. If they aren't freed by design, these urban basements will remain fragments of the underworld; as dark and threatening as the realms of the unknown are to the mentally handicapped.

This architect has been more concerned with museums than with any other building type one could think of. The proportion of museums within the list of his projects and buildings realized is extremely high, even if one allows for the fact that exhibition and museum projects represented a higher percentage of public building during the last decade than in many previous years. Axel Schultes continually took the opportunities offered by suitable competitions in the Federal Republic: a Haus der Geschichte for Berlin and for Stuttgart, the Seville World Fair, the Bonn Museums in Friedrich-Ebert-Allee, the ethnological museum in Frankfurt. He seems to find a link between museums or exhibition buildings and the 'depth' that he loves. Museums contain things that have come to us from the chasms of the past, from the 'well-springs of time', as Thomas Mann called it, 'where myth is at home and ancient norms and ancient forms of life are founded'. Schultes' designs respond to depths of time with depths of space; they urge the visitor to take a momentary 'journey into the pit'. The way down through geological strata is the way back into history. History ('Geschichte') is taken literally as something presented layer ('Schicht') upon layer. Axel Schultes does the same thing in this book. He digs his way from the surface, 1991, back into his own biography.

In a large number of designs Schultes creates an impression of hollowing out, chipping, and passing through gorges even in broad daylight. The International Forum in Tokyo, the Maritime Court in Hamburg, the library in Alexandria, museums in Bonn, Frankfurt and Berlin are examples in which exterior wings, side sections or roof surfaces draw the outlines of a preordained whole. An impression is given of massive overall volume that can only be made useful by subtraction. Spaces seem to be formed not by adding parts, but by processing a whole which is at first undivided, a block of stone or a cylindrical shape. The design process seems sculptural, the block of stone is continually reduced in substance as parts are taken and the intended figure revealed. In the history of building this subtractive process has been used in a variety of places and at a variety of times, not just in imagination, but in reality: in the Chinese loess belt, where buildings and courtyards were cut from layers of

San Nicola in Bari

in Hamburg, die alexandrinische Bibliothek, die Bonner, Frankfurter und Berliner Museen sind Beispiele, bei denen Aussenflügel, Seitentrakte oder Dachflächen die Konturen eines vorgegebenen Ganzen ziehen. Es entsteht der Eindruck eines massiven Gesamtvolumens, das erst durch Subtraktionen der Nutzbarkeit zugeführt wird. Räume scheinen sich nicht aus der addierenden Zusammenstellung von Teilen zu ergeben, sondern durch die Bearbeitung eines zunächst ungeteilten Ganzen, eines Quaders oder einer Zylinderform. Der Entwurfsvorgang wirkt wie ein bildhauerischer Prozess, bei dem der Steinblock durch Wegnehmen immer weiter in seiner materiellen Substanz vermindert wird und dabei die beabsichtigten Figuren freigelegt werden. In der Baugeschichte ist dieses subtraktive Verfahren an den unterschiedlichsten Orten und zu den unterschiedlichsten Zeiten nicht nur fiktiv, im Als-ob, sondern realiter angewendet worden: im Lössgürtel Nordchinas, wo Häuser und Höfe in die Erdschicht geschnitten wurden, oder in Anatolien oder der Provence mit ihren in die Felsen geschlagenen Behausungen. Die äthiopische Feldkirche über kreuzförmigem Grundriss, die aus dem Gestein abgelöst und ausgehöhlt wurde, könnte ohne weiteres in einem der vertieften Baugründe von Schultes stehen. An den berühmten Nollischen Stadtplan von Rom aus dem Jahre 1748 erinnert Schultes' Gutachten für die Berliner Friedrichstrasse, das Vorschläge über die drei zur Diskussion gestellten Baublöcke hinaus machte, oder sein Beitrag für das Terrain zwischen Güterbahnhof und Messe in Frankfurt. Wie die römischen Kupferstecher hat Schultes aus dem architektonischen Gegenstand, dem Block oder Palast, die öffentlich zugänglichen Flächen herausgelöst. Das Objekt wird zur Matrix von Stadtraum.

Wo Schultes nicht unter, sondern über der Erde arbeitet, ist ein Motiv für ihn unentbehrlich, das er selbst die 'Grosse Wand' genannt hat. Die umfassende, geschlossene Mauer, rechtwinklig, kreisförmig oder ellipsoid, fingiert den positiven Block, aus dem die Negative der Räume gewonnen werden. Sie übt Schutzfunktion in zweierlei Hinsicht aus. Sie schirmt die Innenwelt, die störanfälligen Vorgänge des Betrachtens, Prüfens, Meditierens, Ruhens, Arbeitens vor den Belästigungen der profanen Aussenwelt ab. Aber die Grosse Wand hält auch die konfliktreichen Begegnungen unterschiedlicher Formen und Gestalten auf dem begrenzten Terrain des Bauplatzes zusammen. Sie bewahrt sozusagen das innere Chaos vor dem äusseren und umgekehrt. Wäre es nach Schultes gegangen, so hätte sich die Hochwand des Bonner Kunstmuseums in einer ebensolchen Wand der Bundeskunsthalle fortgesetzt. Abschirmung und Umgrenzung stellen einen profanen Temenos oder, weniger feierlich gesagt: eine Karawanserei her, hinter deren Mauern sich die inneren Abläufe ungestört entwickeln können. 'Wie anders als in der Abblendung des Draussen soll der Besucher die Konzentration aufbringen!'

Dass in solchen zeitgenössischen Varianten der alten Stadt- oder Klostermauer heutzutage auch ein Moment der Resignation liegt, ist offenkundig. Wie die alten Gemeinwesen sich gegen Feinde und Wegelagerer absicherten, so die neuen Bauanlagen gegen Verkehrslärm und Emissionen. Der öffentliche Bau verzichtet aktiv in die Öffentlichkeit hineinzuwirken; er stellt statt dessen Enklaven zur Verfügung. An der Bun-

San Nicola in Bari

Blarney Castle, Cork, Ireland

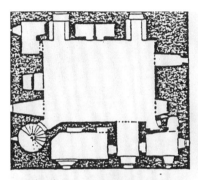
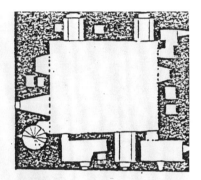
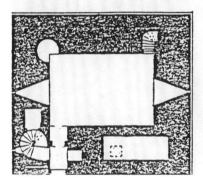
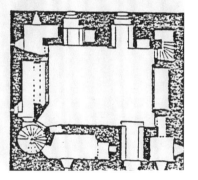

desstrasse 9 in Bonn, einer der desolatesten Stadtstrassen der Republik, war in den Augen des Architekten offenbar nicht mehr viel zu retten. Die Mauer des Kunstmuseums gibt ihr zwar an der westlichen Seite eine Fassung, aber zugleich unterbleibt die Wechselrede von Bau und Strassenraum. Die kaputte Stadt ist nicht von einzelnen Architekten und mit einem einzelnen Gebäude in Ordnung zu bringen. So stellt Schultes wenigstens ein umgrenztes Spielfeld her, auf dem seine Regeln gelten oder gelten könnten. Geht die Natur nicht ähnlich vor? Auch sie sorgt für die Leibeshülle, die Zellblasen und Pneus, die Häute und Kokons, die Panzer und Schalen, die der Innerlichkeit der Lebewesen Schutz gewähren.

Aber nein, die organische Metapher stimmt im Falle dieses Architekten nicht. Schultes entwirft keine organische Architektur. Die inneren Organe schmiegen sich nicht weich ineinander, wie es die der Lebewesen in ihren Körperhöhlen tun. Bei Schultes stossen sich vielmehr die Dinge hart im umgrenzten Raum, überschneiden, ja durchdringen sich. Dreieckige, kreis- oder ellipsenförmige Grossformen sind, manchmal auch nur in angedeuteteten Restverläufen, auf rechtwinklige Strukturen projiziert und erzeugen mit ihnen eine kollisionsreiche Nachbarschaft. Wie wichtig ihm die klärende geometrische Figur ist, erweist sich vor allem dort, wo er sie nachträglich der vorhandenen Substanz aufprägt wie beim Berliner Hauptsitz der Deutschen Bank. In der Folge der Grundrissbilder, vom Untergeschoss bis zu den letzten Obergeschossen, tritt die Kreisform hervor wie bei der allmählichen Entschlüsselung einer an-

earth, or in Anatolia or Provence where houses are cut out of rock. The Ethiopian field church on a cruciform ground plan, detached from and hollowed out of the rock, could easily be in the depths of one of Schultes' buildings. Both, Schultes' study on the Friedrichstrasse in Berlin, which includes a larger area than the discussion initially was to contain, and the site between the freight station and exhibition grounds in Frankfurt, resembled the 1748 town plan of Rome by Nolli. Similar to the works of the roman engraver, Schultes has separated common grounds out of the architectural object, city block or palace for instance, therefore making the objects matrices of urban space.

When Schultes works above, rather than below ground, there is one motif that he cannot do without, that he has himself called the Great Wall. An embracing, closed wall, right-angled, circular or ellipsoid, creates the positive block from which the negative element, rooms, can be gained. It has a protective function in two ways. It screens the inner world, procedures susceptible to interference like considering, testing, meditating, resting, working, from the unwelcome attentions of a profane outside world. But the Great Wall also holds together conflict-rich encounters between different forms and shapes on the restricted terrain of a building site. It protects inner chaos from outer chaos, and vice versa. If Schultes had had his way, the high wall of the Bonn Kunstmuseum would have been continued by just such a wall in the Kunsthalle. Screening off and enclosure create a profane temenos or, put less solemnly, a caravanserai, behind the walls of which the internal order of events can run its course undisturbed. 'How else can a visitor concentrate except by blocking out the outside world!'

It is obvious that there is an element of resignation as well in such contemporary variations on the old town or monastery wall. Just as old communities protected themselves from enemies and highwaymen, modern buildings protect us against traffic noise and atmospheric pollution. Public building denies itself active impact on the public; instead it places enclaves at our disposal. Alongside Bundesstrasse 9 in Bonn, one of the most desolate urban streets in the Republic, Schultes apparently could not find much more to save. The wall of the Kunstmuseum did give it a border on its western side, but there is no dialogue between building and street. A wrecked town cannot be restored to order by an individual architect or a single building. So Schultes creates an enclosed playing area in which his rules are valid or could be valid. Does not nature act in a similar way? It too provides body covering, cellular bubbles and tyres, skins and cocoons, armour and shells that protect the inwardness of living things.

But no, the organic metaphor is not correct in the case of this architect. Schultes does not design organic architecture. Internal organs do not nestl softly against each other, as they do within the body cavities of living things. In Schultes' work things are more inclined to collide in enclosed space, cut across each other, even interpenetrate. Large triangular, circular or elliptical shapes are projected, sometimes only as a hint of the end of a figure, on to right-angled structures, and produce collision-rich proximity. The importance to him of clarifying geometrical shapes is clear when examining his addition to existing structures, such

die große Moschee in Cordoba

the grand mosque in Cordoba

fangs unsichtbaren Geheimschrift. Gelegentlich ergeben sich Grundrissbilder, als habe einer ein rundes Vergrösserungsglas oder eine dicke dreieckige Glasfläche auf den Plan gelegt. An den Rändern brechen sich die Linien (Mauerzüge, Korridore), ohne in ihrem Richtungszug beeinträchtigt zu werden; darunter treten, wie unter einer Vergrösserung, andere Strukturen zutage. Hätte man sich für Schultes einen anderen Beruf auszudenken, so könnte es der eines Präparators oder eines Chirurgen sein – jedenfalls nicht der eines Gärtners, als den sich andere seiner Kollegen gerne sehen. Das Hegen und Pflegen, die freundliche Geste, das Umgrünen und Dekorieren der Lücken und Zäsuren ist nicht seine Sache.

Die städtebaulichen Aufgaben, denen er sich in den letzten Jahren stellte, waren auch nicht danach angetan. Die Abraumhalden in Gelsenkirchen, der Güterbahnhof in Frankfurt, auch die städtischen Ödflächen in Berlin-Mitte oder – besonders heikel und mit Emotionen besetzt – in Dresden provozierten ihn zu rigorosen Antworten. Da werden harte Kanten gezogen, Strukturen befestigt oder neu geschaffen, ordnende Figuren implantiert, neue Konventionen gesetzt. Manchmal scheint es, als stellten sich die grossen Städte diesem Architekten als ein Urwald dar, in den er mit der Machete Platz zum Leben und zum Atmen schlagen müsste. Die Abweichungen von der strikten Regel und die versöhnende Unordnung würden sich schon von selbst wieder einstellen.

Hinter der Arbeit von Axel Schultes steht die Ästhetik des Widerspruchs, des Konflikts, der Collage. Zu ihr haben sich in diesem Jahrhundert die Bildenden Künstler bekannt, als die Architekten noch immer die alten Träume vom stellvertretenden Weltbaumeister, vom gottähnlichen Schöpfer universaler Harmonien träumten. Erst Claude Lévi-Strauss' Preislied auf den Bricoleur, der mit Hilfe vorhandenen Materials seine Erfindungen bastelt, Robert Venturis Entdeckung von Komplexität und Widerspruch, Colin Rowes Rechtfertigung des Fragments und der Collage im Städtebau waren Absagen an die Grosse Formel, die alles regeln sollte. Das 'Ganze' wurde 'schwierig', wie Venturi es formulierte. Und ist das 'Schwierige' nicht die tägliche Erfahrung des Architekten? Was unten weite Räume für öffentliche oder kommerzielle Geschäfte verlangt, benötigt oben die engmaschige Zellenstruktur für Wohnungen oder Büros; was auf der einen Seite eine vitale Geschäftsstrasse flankiert, ist auf der anderen kostbarem historischen Bestand konfrontiert. Mit den Absurditäten, die Geschichte und Gegenwart angesammelt hatten, musste man umzugehen lernen. Sie kurieren zu wollen, hiesse sie zu verschlimmern. Diese Botschaft hat viele jüngere Architekten erreicht.

Entsprechend wurden die Vorbilder ausgetauscht. Nicht das repräsentative Paris Ludwigs XIV., dem Le Corbusier noch seine Hochachtung zollte, oder der barocke Urbanismus mit seinen grossen Ordnungsfiguren, den Sigfried Giedion an den Beginn seines Modernismus-Klassikers *Raum, Zeit, Architektur* stellte, gaben die Muster her. Nun waren es die Planungen an den Grenzen zur scheinbaren Nichtplanung, bei denen die partiellen Lösungen keiner Gesamtlösung mehr gehorchten. Die Bautenkollektion Kaiser Hadrians wurde interessanter als das achsenstreng geordnete Rom Papst Sixtus' V., der Crash-Kurs interessanter als die

as the extension to the headquarters of the Deutsche Bank in Berlin. Like deciphering an invisible secret code, the circular form became apparent in the development of the plans from the basement to the top floors. Occasionally images appear that look as though someone had put a round magnifying glass or a thick, triangular piece of glass down on the ground plan. Lines break at the edges (runs of wall, corridors) without their fundamental direction being affected; and amidst all this other structures come to light, as if magnified. If you had to think of a different profession for Schultes, you would probably come upon a taxidermist or surgeon; but never a landscape designer as other architects would like to consider themselves. Fussy care and bother, polite friendliness, the decoration and lavishing of gaps and caesuras is certainly not for him.

The urban problems, that he was presented with in the last few years also had to be dealt with rigorously: mining dumps in Gelsenkirchen, the freight station in Frankfurt, urban wasteland in the centre of Berlin, and, particularly delicate and highly emotional, Dresden provoked him to rigorous responses. Decisive lines were made, structures were strengthened or newly erected, defining figures implanted, new conventions established. It seems as if cities were sometimes jungles to the architect, which he had to cut down with a machete to create space to breathe and move about. Deviations of strict rules and the forgiving disorder are left to reappear on their own.

Behind Axel Schultes' work lie the aesthetics of contradiction, of conflict, of collage. Fine artists professed their faith in this aesthetic in this century, while architects were still dreaming their dreams of being deputy architect of the world, of god-like creation of universal harmony. The first negations of the Great Formula to solve everything were Claude Lévi-Strauss' hymn of praise to the bricoleur who put together his inventions with the help of available materials, Robert Venturi's discovery of complexity and contradiction, Colin Rowe's defence of fragment and collage in urban planning. The 'whole' became 'difficult', as Venturi put it. And is 'difficulty' not the architect's daily experience? Down below he needs broad spaces for public or commercial operations, then a closely-meshed cell structure for flats or offices above; something that is flanked on one side by a lively shopping street faces valuable historical stock on the other. We have to learn to live with the absurdities accumulated by past and present. Wanting to cure them only makes them worse. This message reached a lot of young architects.

Models were changed appropriately. Thinking was no longer based on ,the imposing Paris of Louis XIV, to which Le Corbusier still paid homage, or baroque urbanism with its great figures of order, which Sigfried Giedion placed at the beginning of his great classic of Modernism, *Raum, Zeit, Architektur*. Now planning was on the borders of non-planning, where partial solutions are no longer subject to an overall solution. The Emperor Hadrian's collection of buildings became more interesting than the rigorous axes of Pope Sixtus V's Rome, collision courses more interesting than universal control. Ultimately attempts at global solutions had come to grief beyond the specialist discipline, in politics and world economics, in international supply and disposal problems. Why should

die Hofmauer der Djoser-Bezirks in Sakkara the courtyard wall of the Djoser district in Sakkara

universale Steuerung. Schliesslich waren globale Lösungsversuche auch jenseits der Fachdisziplin, in Politik und Weltwirtschaft, bei den internationalen Ver- und Entsorgungsproblemen gescheitert. Warum sollten sich Architekten und Planer zumuten, was Kollegen anderer Ressorts missglückt war?

Auch mit solchen Einsichten kann man unterschiedlich umgehen. Die Mischung des Heterogenen, des kunsthistorisch Abgesegneten wie des Ordinär-Trivialen, war kein Weg für Axel Schultes. Das populistische Mischangebot ist nicht sein Fall. Schultes hat sein Repertoire begrenzt. Er kennt Lieblingsmotive und scheut sich nicht, sie in wechselnder Zuordnung und morphologischer Verwandlung mehrfach einzusetzen. Die frei geführte oder geometrisch geregelte Terrassierung als hängender Garten oder Amphitheater gehört dazu; der Trichter als Raumform, als Stützenkapitell oder sogar als Beleuchtungskörper; der bauwerkshöhe Anschnitt als Fuge, Schlitz oder Schlucht; vor allem die Neigung zu zentralen Raumkonzepten. Längsrechteckige Grundrisse offenbaren sich bei Schultes oft als eine Verkettung mehrerer Zentralgrundrisse. In der Verwendung dieser Motive treten gewollte Ambivalenzen auf. Die drei-, vier- oder mehrbeinigen, von flachen Platten gedeckten Gebilde lassen sich als 'Tisch' wie als Stadtloggia lesen. Auch hier tritt ein Alice-in-Wonderland-Effekt ein. Die Dinge wirken als 'riesig' oder als 'normal' je nach der Interpretation des Betrachters.

Die Massnahmen, mit denen Schultes die Unversehrtheit eines geometrischen Grossgebildes aufhebt, führen paradoxerweise nicht dazu, dass ein Ganzes in seine Teile zerfällt. Denn gerade in der Verletzung wird die verletzte Figur deutlich. Die Durchstossung von Halb- oder Vollkreisen mit Achsen, die nicht durch den Kreismittelpunkt geführt sind, oft auch nicht lotrecht auf den sonstigen Achsen des Grundrissystems stehen, inszeniert Kreisform und Axialität, statt sie zu annullieren. Die Diagonale, die im Grundriss und manchmal auch im Schnitt das Quadrat zerschneidet, lässt neue Figuren entstehen, ohne die alten vergessen zu machen. Ein anspruchsvolles Niveau wird bei allen diesen Manipulationen eingehalten. Die jeweiligen Störungen dramatisieren, aber das Drama ist keine postmoderne Verkleidungskomödie. Mehr als die Formen, so scheint es, interessieren diesen Architekten die Räume, die sie erzeugen. Ein gewisses Pathos haftet sämtlichen Entwürfen an.

Wo lernt man eine Sprache wie diese, die Ansprüche an Juroren, Bauherren und Nutzer stellt, die ungewöhnliche Raumerlebnisse verspricht und bequeme Nachlässigkeit nicht duldet? Schultes hat 1969–72 bei Josef Paul Kleihues gearbeitet, in den Jahren, als das Büro mit der Hauptwerkstatt der Berliner Stadtreinigung beschäftigt war. Auch Kleihues kennt Präfigurationen. Er liebt es, seinen preussischen Rationalismus durch systemwidrige Anhängsel oder abgewinkelte Achsen zu stören und zu poetisieren. Aber wo Schultes seine Bauten in den märkischen Sand (oder in welche Erdformationen auch immer) einwurzeln lässt, wo er seine Grundrissfiguren äussersten Spannungen aussetzt und den Raum immer wieder nach seinem Sinn und seinen Möglichkeiten befragt, hält Kleihues es mit einer serenen schinkelesken Klassizität. Dagegen gibt es Projekte von Louis Kahn, an die Schultes-Entwürfe erinnern können. Im Hof des Dominikanerinnenklosters in Media, Pennsyl-

architects and planners be expected to do things that colleagues in other departments had failed to master?

There are various ways of dealing with insights of this kind as well. Axel Schultes was not interested in mixing heterogeneous things, things blessed by art historians, or the vulgar and trivial. He is not a man for the populist mixture. Schultes restricted his repertoire. He has favourite motifs and is not afraid to use them in various combinations and morphological transformations. One of these is freestyle or geometrically controlled terracing as hanging garden or amphitheatre; funnels as spatial forms, as support capitals or even light fittings; an incision running the full height of the building as crack, slit or gorge; above all an inclination to a centralized conception of space. In Schultes' work longitudinal rectangular ground plans often turn out to be a chain of centrally-organized ground plans. Deliberate ambivalence is created by the use of these motifs. Structures with three, four or more legs covered with flat slabs can be read as 'tables' or as urban loggias. Here too there is an Alice in Wonderland effect. Things seems 'gigantic' or 'normal' according to the viewer's interpretation.

Schultes' devices for doing away with the intactness of a large geometrical structure paradoxically do not cause the whole to be fragmented into its parts. The disturbance is the very thing that makes the disturbed figure clear. Semi- or full circles breaking through axes that do not go through the centre of the circle and are often not perpendicular to other axes of the base system make a setting for circularity and axiality, rather than annulling them. The diagonal that cuts the square in the floor plan and sometimes also in section causes new figures to emerge without letting us forget the old ones. All these manipulations take place at a sophisticated level. The disturbances cause drama in each case, but it is not the drama of Post-Modern fancy-dress comedy. It seems that this architect is less interested in shapes than in the spaces they create. All the designs are imbued with a certain drama.

How does one learn a language like this, that makes demands on competition judges, clients and users, that promises unusual experiences of space and will not put up with comfortable carelessness? From 1969 to 1972 Schultes worked with Josef Paul Kleihues, in the years when his office was working on the main workshops of the Berlin municipal cleansing department. Kleihues is familiar with archetypes as well. He likes breaking and poeticizing his Prussian rationalism with appendages that do not fit in with the system, or with bent axes. But where Schultes lets his buildings take root in the sand of the Mark (or whatever other kind of ground), exposes his base shapes to extreme tension and continually questions space about its meaning and its possibilities, Kleihues clings to Schinkelesque classicism. On the other hand there are projects by Louis Kahn that could be reminiscent of designs by Schultes. In the courtyard the Dominican nunnery in Media, Pennsylvania, a project dating from 1965–68, the convent buildings are enclosed and protected from centrifugal force by a Great Wall of the kind that Schultes loves. Kahn too approved of poeticizing building – and not only approved of it, but achieved it: 'Art is a form that fills order with life'.

Behind Kahn stands Le Corbusier, whose *Œuvre complète* still condie Umfassungsmauer des Djoser-Bezirks in Sakkara   the outer wall of the Djoser district in Sakkara

vania, einem Projekt von 1965–68, treiben die Baukörper des Konvents, eingefasst und vor zentrifugalen Kräften bewahrt durch eine Grosse Wand, wie Schultes sie liebt. Auch Kahn hat eine Poetisierung des Bauens befürwortet – und nicht nur befürwortet, sondern realisiert: 'Kunst ist eine Form, die Ordnung mit Leben füllt.'

Hinter Kahn steht Le Corbusier, dessen *Œuvre complète* auch für die Enkelgeneration noch Inspiration genug enthält. Die Rechteckschnecke seines 'Musée à la croissance illimitée' kehrt, in der Diagonalen aufgetrennt, in Schultes' Werk wieder. Le Corbusier hat die 'Freiheit der Füllung' vorexerziert, die Wahlmöglichkeiten, die ein umgrenztes Geviert erlaubt. Im Werk der zwanziger Jahre sind es die 'compositions cubiques' seiner Villen, die in den anspruchsvollsten Beispielen wie der Villa Savoye die Aushöhlung eines vorgegebenen plastischen Volumens demonstrieren. Im Spätwerk zeigt der Klosterhof von La Tourette (1957 bis 60), wie 'confrontation' und 'synthèse' zusammengehen. Und hinter den Meistern des 20. Jahrhunderts stehen die Leistungen früherer Jahrhunderte, die anonymen eher als die an Namen geketteten: die Grundrisse mauerstarker mittelalterlicher Wehrtürme mit ihren scheinbar in die Substanz eingeschnittenen Treppenspindeln, Scharten und Gelassen; die Moschee von Cordoba, deren Schiffe aus aufgesetzten Laternen geheimnisreiches Licht empfangen; die Grosse Wand um den Tempelbezirk des Königs Djoser in Sakkara; die Kragsteingewölbe ägyptischer Grabkammern; das Osireion, die gebaute Insel im unterirdischen Gewässer von Abydos.

Fast alle Entwürfe dieses Bandes sind in Wettbewerben entstanden. Projekte wie die von Axel Schultes haben gute Chancen für Auszeichnungen. Aber sie haben es schwer, den ersten Preis zu erringen. Was Schultes vorlegt, gilt als hochinteressant, schwierig und radikal. Seine Entwürfe rückhaltlos zu empfehlen, muss eine Jury ihren ganzen Mut zusammennehmen. Projekte, über die sich Kompromisse schliessen lassen, haben es leichter in den gruppendynamischen Prozessen, die Jurysitzungen darstellen. Schultes dagegen ist ein Anwärter für zweite und dritte Preise oder für Sonderankäufe. Das mag Genugtuung verschaffen, aber es verschafft nur selten Aufträge. Beim Wettbewerb für das Deutsche Historische Museum war Schultes für viele der eigentliche Gewinner, der geheime Sieger. Aber der erste Preis ging an einen Entwurf, dessen Handschrift internationales Prestige versprach, der zweite an ein Projekt von einfacher Lesbarkeit. Gebaut wurde nach der Vereinigung der Stadthälften keiner.

Mit Dietrich Bangert, Bernd Jansen und Stefan Scholz arbeitete Axel Schultes seit 1972 zusammen. Innerhalb des Teams steht jeder für seine eigenen Projekte ein, der Drang zur Selbständigkeit unter dem gemeinsamen Dach war unverkennbar und hat im vergangenen Jahr zur Trennung geführt. Eine neue Partnerschaft firmiert unter Schultes' Namen. Was Schultes entwirft und manchmal baut, hat über die Jahre hinweg beschreibbare Eigenart gewonnen und bewahrt. Es ist ein erworbener Vorrat von Konzepten und Formen, der dem raschen Wechsel der Moden und Standpunkte widersteht, Gepäck und Kompass für die nächste Wegstrecke.

Wolfgang Pehnt

tains inspiration enough for the generation of his grandsons. The rectangular snail of his 'Musée à la croissance illimitée' returns, opened on the diagonal, in Schultes' work. Le Corbusier had exercised 'freedom of filling', the range of choices permitted by an enclosed square. In his work in the twenties it was the 'compositions cubiques' of his villas, which in the most sophisticated examples like the Villa Savoye demonstrate the hollowing out of a given three-dimensional volume. In his later work the monastery courtyard of La Tourette (1957–60) shows how 'confrontation' and 'synthèse' go together. And behind the masters of the twentieth century are the achievements of earlier centuries, anonymous ones rather than the great names: wall-thick medieval fortress towers with their newels, embrasures and dungeons apparently carved out of the substance of the building; the mosque at Cordoba, its aisles bathed in mysterious light from lanterns on the top; the Great Wall around the temple precinct of King Djoser in Saqqara; the corbelled vaults of Egyptian burial chambers; the Osireion, the artificial island in the subterranean waters of Abydos.

Almost all the designs in this book were produced for competitions. Projects like Axel Schultes' have a good chance of receiving awards, but it is difficult for them to win first prize. What Schultes offers is highly interesting, difficult and radical. A panel of judges would need all their courage to recommend his designs unreservedly. Projects about which compromises can be made have more chance in group dynamic processes like those which happen among competition judges. Schultes is more of a candidate for second or third prize or for special purchases. This may be grounds for satisfaction, but it seldom produces commissions. In the competition for the Deutsches Historisches Museum Schultes was the real winner for many, the secret victor. But the first prize went to a design of which the handwriting promised more international prestige, the second to a project that was easy to read. After the unification of the city none of the projects were built.

Axel Schultes worked with Dietrich Bangert, Bernd Jansen and Stefan Scholz from 1972. Within the team each man takes responsibility for his own projects, the urge to be independent under the communal roof was unmistakable and led to separation last year. A new partnership is now operating under Schultes' name. What Schultes designs and sometimes builds has gained and retained recognizable individuality over the years. It is an acquired stock of concepts and forms resistant to rapid changes of fashion and points of view, it is luggage and compass for the next stage of the journey.

Wolfgang Pehnt

Potsdamer Bahnhof, Berlin

1991, Axel Schultes

'Die Bahnhöfe sind die Stadttore der Neuzeit' – den Autozubringern, unseren wahren Stadttoren, den Verkehr abzugraben, die Bahnhöfe wieder in Front zu bringen, hier, am 'Potsdamer Platz', kann man anfangen: warum nicht auch den ICE hier halten lassen, *einen* Knoten wenigstens schürzen mit S- und U-Bahnen, den Regionalzügen und den Bussen? Der Lehrter Fernbahnhof irgendwo hinterm Spreebogen – warum, wenn man hier unterm Potsdamer schon fast alles liegen hat?

Im Nachgang zum Wettbewerb entstand ein Vorschlag zur Neuordnung dieses in seiner Bedeutung kaum zu unterschätzenden zentralen Verkehrsknotenpunkts mit seiner ja auch direkten Auswirkung auf die anstehenden Hochbaumassnahmen. Wie beim rigiden, zeitlich und finanziell sehr aufwendigen Vorschlag im Wettbewerb verzichtet auch dieses Konzept nicht auf die vor allem räumlich grosszügige Integration aller Verkehrssysteme, verwendet aber alle vorhandenen Bahntrassen und gibt, mit der präzisen Beschränkung auf die Unterbauung nur der Leipziger Strasse, den Weg frei für die privaten Baumassnahmen in unmittelbarer Nachbarschaft.

Diese zentrale Bahnhofsterrasse, Variante und Verdoppelung des darüberliegenden Strassenprofils, bindet und orientiert mit ihren etwa 400 Metern Länge alle Verkehrsströme der Passarellen – mit den diesen Hallenraum durchstossenden Bahnsteigen und dem vielfältigen Nutzungsangebot bis hinunter zur neuen U-Bahn-Trasse auf -21.00 m könnte das schöne Wort von der 'Mutterhöhle der Bahnhöfe' wieder und wörtlicher Raum weden.

Die Stadt ist hier in der Verantwortung, diese Aufgabe nicht nur verkehrstechnisch zu erledigen, sondern diesen Ort in neuer und inspirierender Gestalt entstehen zu lassen, den Mythos des Ortes wenigstens unterhalb des Stadthorizontes neu zu begründen, allem Hick-Hack um die 'Neue Stadt' darüber zum Trotz.

'Stations are the city gates of modern age' – dig the traffic out of the motorway feeder roads, our real city gates, bring the stations up front again: why not make the Inter-City Express trains stop here as well, tie at least *one* knot with commuter and underground trains, with regional trains and buses? The Lehrter Bahnhof as a long-distance station somewhere beyond the Spree bend – why, when there's almost everything here, under Potsdamer Platz?

Subsequently to the competition a suggestion was made for a new arrangement of this supremely important central traffic junction, which also has a direct effect on the imminent high-rise building programme. As in the rigid proposal of the competition, expensive in terms of both time and money, this concept as well does not sacrifice generous integration of all traffic systems, particularly in spatial terms. But it uses all the available railway lines and, by restriction to building only under the Leipziger Strasse, leaves the way clear for private building in the immediate vicinity.

This central Station terrace, variant and double of the street profile above it, is about 400 metres long and connects and directs all the traffic streams from the passarelles – with all the platforms thrusting through the hall, and the broad range of use right down to the new underground line at -21.00 metres, the beautifull idea of the 'mothercave of all stations' could become space again, literally.

Here the city is responsible for carrying out the task not just in terms of traffic, it also has to recreate this place in new and inspiring form, and reestablish its myth, at least below the city horizon, in defiance of all the bickering about the 'New City' above it.

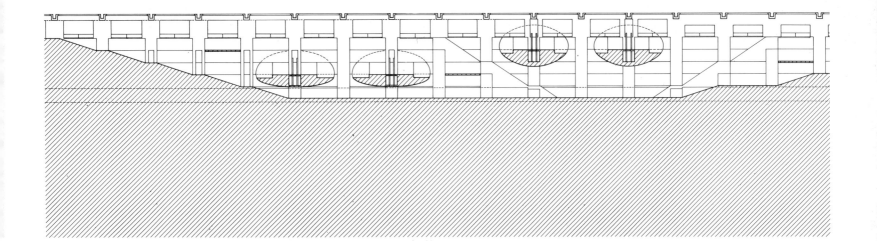

Potsdamer Platz, Berlin

1991, Axel Schultes
in Bangert Jansen Scholz Schultes
mit Charlotte Frank

Der Potsdamer Platz, mittlerweile zum 'Herzen Deutschlands' hochstilisiert, soll er wirklich das werden, was er niemals war: Platz? Kluge Menschen, Nicht-Architekten natürlich, möchten den Ort retten, so wie er geworden ist – nach ein paar Jahren vor allem deutscher Geschichte: wüst und leer. Aber Berlin, auch Berlin hinter dem Kulturforum, wird wieder sein, der Potsdamer Kreuzweg wird wieder materiale Gestalt annehmen, wird so oder so in Glas und Beton banalisiert auferstehen.

Ob nun in Schmuckplatz-Manier Lennéscher Auffassung Stadtreparatur ins nicht mehr Reparable weitergeführt wird, ob sich vielleicht auch nur vier reisige Bügeleisen entlang der beiden Diagonal-Alleen auf den Strassenstern zuschieben (auch das in der Tradition des Ortes – das Dilemma der Architekten ist hier inspirierenderweise von mephistophelischer Dimension: "drum besser wär's, dass nichts entstünde!"

Östlich der Elbe beginnt die Steppe: angesichts unserer 'Berliner Platzkultur' schleicht sich Wehmut ein: einmal wenigstens in Berlin einen Platz haben, der es in räumlicher Intensität aufnehmen könnte mit seinen südlichen Vorbildern – ein Traum vielleicht für die Spreeinsel, da wo das Schloss einmal stand; hier aber auf der Potsdamer Kreuzung ist *alles* anders: ein Ort gewordener Widerspruch, eine Konfrontation sondergleichen, eine Kollision der dritten, vierten Art will hier ein räumliches Gleichnis finden.

Wie also einen Ram bauen, der keiner ist? wie die Euklidsche Kiste weggeben *und* den 'Raum' behalten oder wie den 'Angriff der Gegenwart', den neuen Raum so dosieren, dass die 'übrige Zeit' dabei nicht auf der Strecke bleibt, die Erinnerung nicht ausgelöscht wird?

Unsere Strategie war dabei die dümmlichste, war vielleicht die einzig mögliche: das eine tun, das andere nicht lassen, Naht und Kluft, Schneise und Kontinuum, Dichte und Durchlässigkeit, Enge und Weite, Randschärfe und -auflösung, Sieb und Topf gleicherweise umsetzen. Platz und Bahnhof fallen dabei in eins, Platzgebäude und Bahnhofshalle ebenso, Platzfläche und Tiergartengrün, Kragdächer und Cafés (die Sonne scheint schräger als der Regen) – die öffentlichen Gebäude am Platz und die Vielfalt ihrer privaten Nutzungen profitieren von der Mehrdeutigkeit dieses Platzraumes. Der Reichstag als nördliche Platzkante und die dreissig Meter Berliner Himmel zwischen den Platzdächern geben die extremen Dimensionen von 'nur mal über die Strasse gehen' und 'ab in die Wälder': für den Potsdamer Platz wenigstens wäre es also nur folgerichtig (und mir sehr lieb), wenn die bösen Zungen recht behielten: die Berliner Plätze sind gar keine!

Das Bebauungsschema der vier neuen Blöcke (Debis, Sony, Wertheim) kehrt die traditionelle Aufgabenteilung von Strasse und Hof um: die mit 'Mall' umschriebenen Galeria-ähnlichen, überglasten Innenhöfe sind die eigentlichen Strassen dieses neuen Quartiers; die Bauwich-artigen Gassen zwischen den Mall-Profilen haben eher dienenden Charakter (Licht, Frischluft, Erschliessung). Es wäre ein Vergnügen, die Wandelbarkeit dieses Bautyps auf die sicher sehr unterschiedlichen Nutzungsvorstellungen der Investoren hin entwurflich zu testen. Bei einer Bauhöhe von 24,00 Metern bzw. ca. 60,00 Metern ist eine GFZ von 5,0 erreichbar.

Potsdamer Platz, Berlin

1991, Axel Schultes
in Bangert Jansen Scholz Schultes
with Charlotte Frank

Potsdamer Platz, now built up into the 'heart of Germany', should it really become something that it never was, a 'Platz', a square? Clever people, non-architects of course, would like to rescue the place as it is now – after a few years of particularly german history: deserted and empty. But Berlin, even Berlin beyond the Kulturforum, will exist again, the Potsdam junction will take material shape again, will rise up again, made banal in glass and concrete, one way or the other.

Whether urban repair in Lenné's decorative square manner is going to be continued into something no longer reparable, whether perhaps just four gigantic irons should push along the two diagonal avenues towards the street-star (this too would be in the tradition of the place) – inspiringly the architect's dilemma is of mephistophelian dimensions here: "and so it would be better that nothing should come forth".

East of the Elbe the steppes begin: as far as our 'Berlin square culture' is concerned, wistful nostalgia is starting to creep in: to have just one square in Berlin that could take on its models in the south as far as spatial intensity is concerned – a dream perhaps for the Spree island, where the Schloss once stood; but here at the Potsdam junction *everything* is different: a contradiction that has become a place, a confrontation beyond compare, a collision of the third, of the fourth kind is trying to find a spatial image here.

So how to build a space that isn't one? How can you give away the Euclidean chest *and* keep the space or how can you treat the 'contemporary attack', the new space in such a way that the 'other times' do not fall by the wayside, and memory is not extinguished?

Our strategy for this was the most stupid possible, was perhaps the only possible one: to do the one thing and not abandon the other, to realize seam and gulf, break and continnum, density and ease of interchange, constriction and space, sharp and blurred edges, sieve and pot in the same manner. This means that square and station become one, and so do the buildings in the square and the station hall, square area and the green of the Tiergarten, cantilever roofs and cafés (the sun shines more obliquely than the rain) – the public buildings in the square and the multiplicity of their private uses profit from the ambiguity of this square space. The Reichstag as the northern extremity of the square and the thirty metres of Berlin sky between the roofs of the square provide the extreme dimensions of 'just nip across the road' and 'off the woods': for Potsdamer Platz at least it would be only logical (and would please me very much) if wicked tongues were proved right: Berlin squares aren't squares at all!

The development scheme for the four new blocks (Debis, Sony, Wertheim) reverses the traditional division of labour for street and courtyard: the inner courtyards, called 'malls', galeria-like and glazed, are the actual streets of the new quarter, the alleys by the mall profiles, like spaces between buildings, are rather more service-like in character (light, fresh, air, access). It would be a pleasure to test the flexibility of this kind of building in design terms against the investors' certainly very varied notions for use. With a building height of 24 m and 60 m respectively a density of 5.0 could be achieved.

Modell des Planungskonzepts   full model of concept

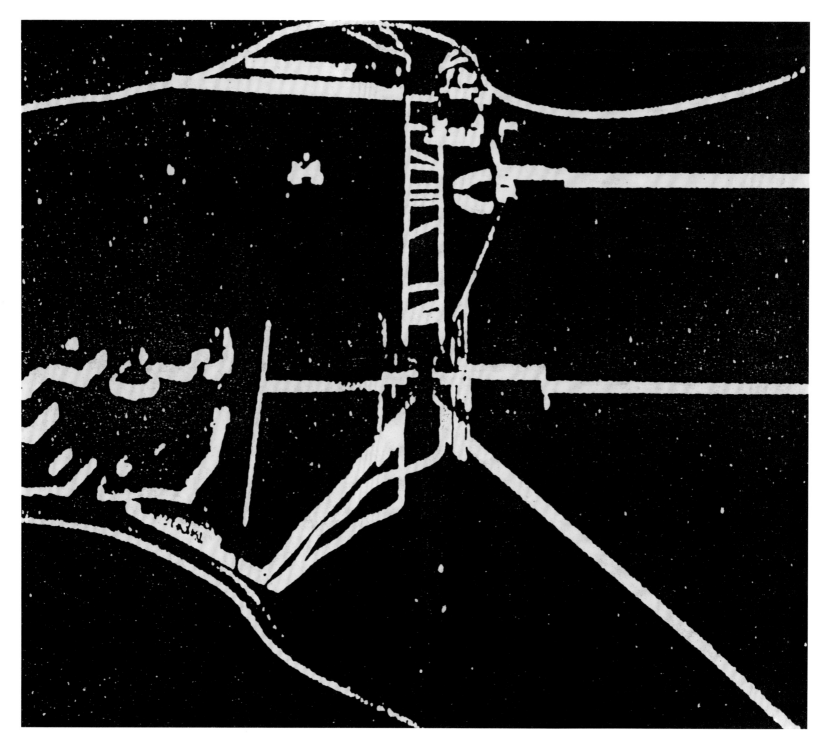

Planungskonzept   concept

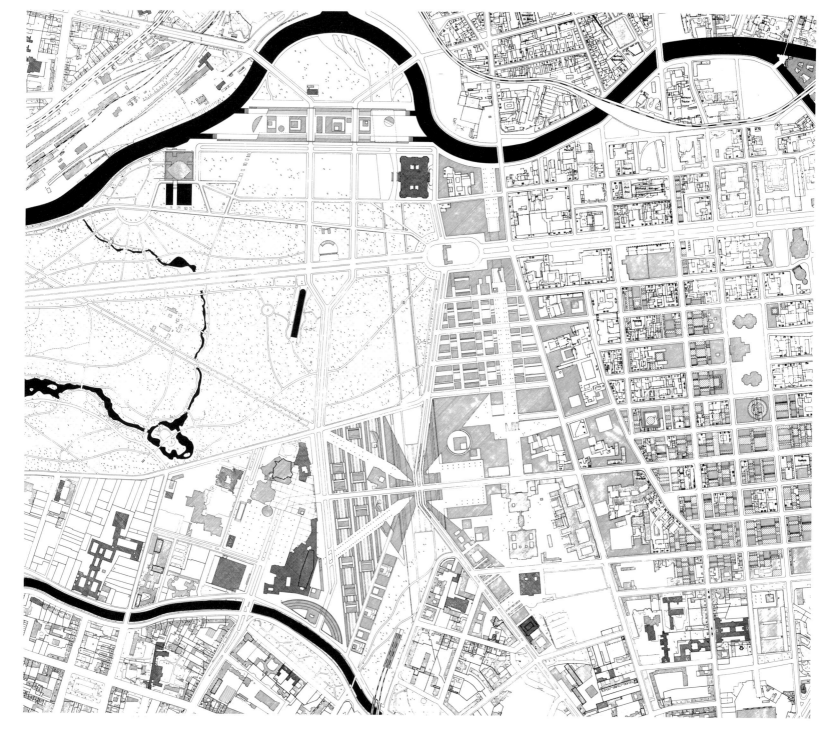

Grundriss Wettbewerbsgebiet
Grundriss Potsdamer Platz

ground plan competition area
ground plan Potsdamer Platz

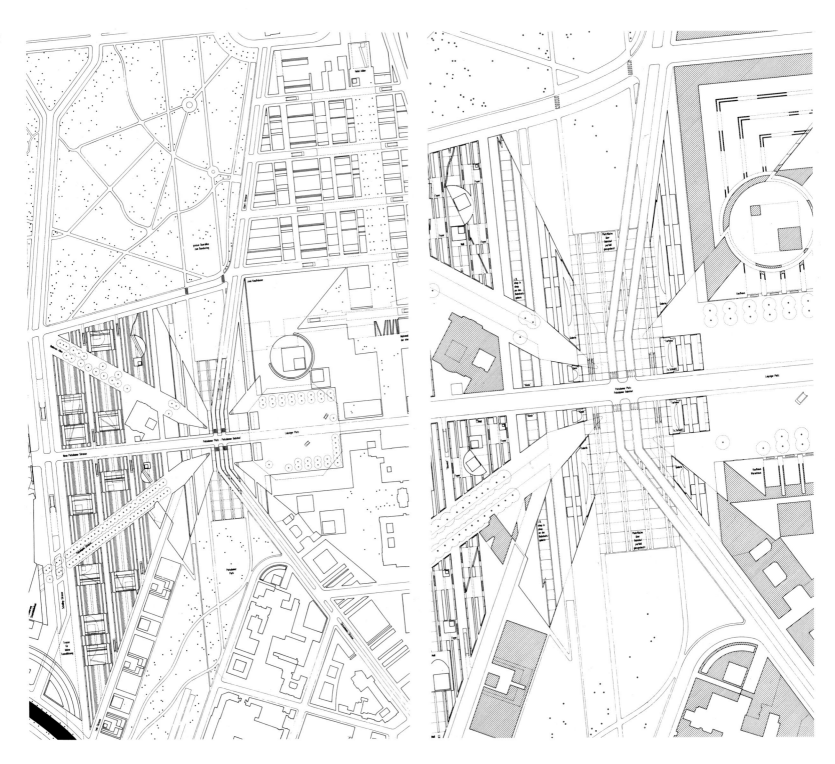

Blick Richtung Tiergarten, von der Stresemannstrasse aus   niew towards Tiergarten, from above Stresemannstrasse

Schnitt durch die neuen Blocks
Schnitt durch Potsdamer Platz und Potsdamer Bahnhof

cross-section through the new blocks
cross-section through Potsdamer Platz and Potsdamer station

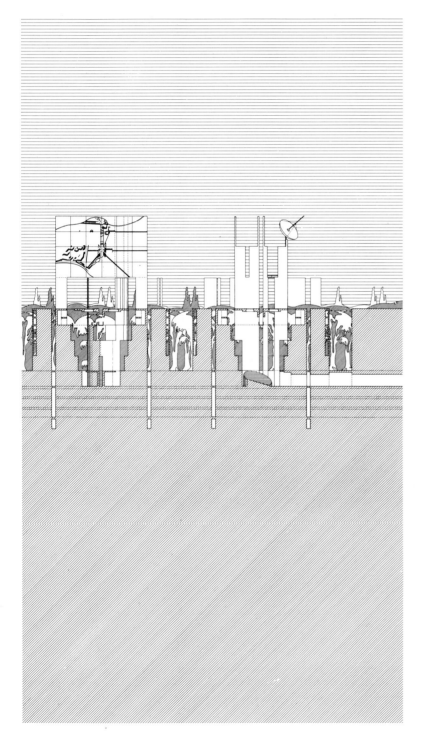
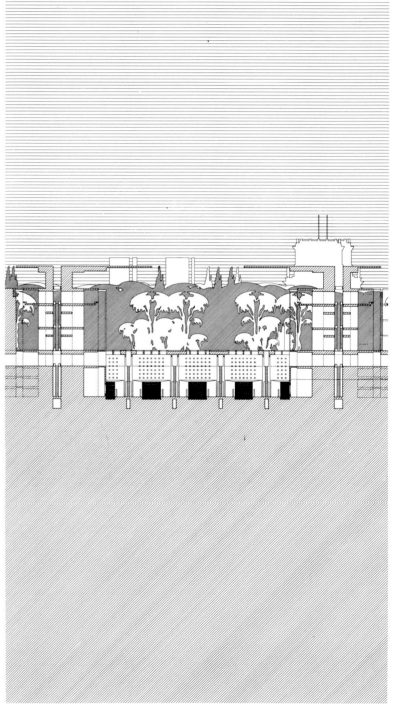

Modellschnitt durch die neuen Blocks   model cross-section through the new blocks

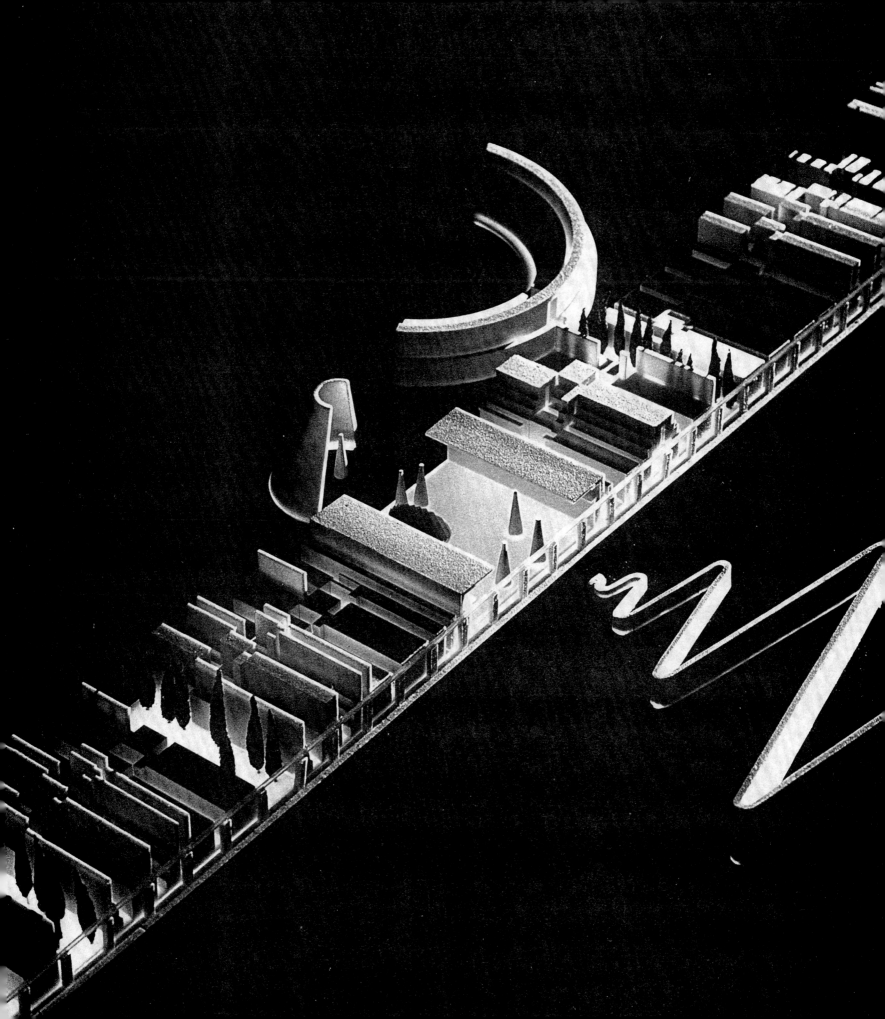

Gewerbepark Gladbeck-Brauck

1991, Axel Schultes
in Bangert Jansen Scholz Schultes
mit Charlotte Frank

Ham se't nich ne Nummer kleener? fragten sich die Architekten angesichts des so gewissenhaft aufgebauten Planungsszenariums, fragt uns jetzt der Entwicklungsträger angesichts unseres Vorschlags zu einem Gewerbe-'Park', der die angemahnte Ausgewogenheit zwischen Stadt und Grün, das Parkartige eben, so deutlich vermissen lässt. Das Vermitteln von Haus und Baum und Strauch und Haus und Baum ... ist unsere Sache nicht, in der architektonischen Grundstruktur nicht, schon gar nicht an einem Ort, der im gestaltlosen Nebeneinander, im blossen Nachvollziehen der Zwänge der Natur, Landwirtschaft, Industrie und Wohnfolge eben nur Siedlung, nicht Ort geworden ist.

Wenn mit einer neuen 'Kultivierungswelle', hier unter der Ägide der IBA, wenn mit einer Industrialisierung der vierten Art, irgendwo zwischen Toyota-Händler und Öko-Tech angesiedelt, Profil für Gladbeck gewonnen werden soll, muss in Dichte, Format, Dimension das noch nicht erkennbare Industriekultur- und Industriebau-Erbe für den aktuellen Zweck ausgebeutet werden.

Es war unsere Aufgabe, die Prämissen der Auslobung auf das tatsächliche Potential der 'Gegend' zu testen und zu korrigieren – gefragt war eine simple, leistungsfähige, planerische Grundstruktur von Erschliessung, Versorgung, Parzellierung und Nutzungsausweisung – das zeigen die Pläne. Gefragt war aber natürlich auch das Bild, die Corporate Identity dieses neuen Stücks Gladbeck, die dem Entwicklungsträger die Brautwerbung, die Akquisition potenter, imageträchtiger Unternehmungen erfolgreich gestalten hilft.

Die Arbeitsmodelle geben, so glaube ich, dieses Bild:
– die straffe Reihung der auf den Parzellen heranwachsenden Büro-, Labor- und Produktionsgebäude bis zu maximal 6 Geschossen in einer Dichte, die sich angesichts des durch Kontaminierung erzwungenen Aufwands rechnet – eine kleine Stadt, nein, nicht in der Stadt, eher 'im Gebeit'. Die festen, nicht zu niedrigen Raumkanten dieses Stadtstreifens, bei aller Durchlässigkeit an den Grün- und Erschliessungsknoten, sind lebenswichtig für das Gelingen dieses Stadt-Bildes;
– das Gelände jenseits dieser Kanten ist Rest, Brache, teilweise durch Gifte zum Niemandsland geworden, vor allem aber Reserve, Vorhaltung: für die Entwicklung grösserer, zusammenhängender Grünflächen, für Sondernutzungen und Sonderbauten, für die Arrondierungen schützenswerter Industriekomplexe.

Nicht die Fortschreibung von Siedlung also, nicht der Park (das Grün in der unmittelbaren Nachbarschaft misst nach Hunderten von Hektar) – eine kompakte, transparente, disziplinierte Reihung von Bauten fast städtischer Struktur knüpft an das industrie-architektonische Erbe aus der ersten, längst vergangenen 'Blütezeit' der Region an.

Gladbeck-Brauck business park

1991, Axel Schultes
in Bangert Jansen Scholz Schultes
with Charlotte Frank

'Aven't they got it a size smaller? the architects wondered when faced with the planning scenario that had been so conscientiously built up, the developers are now wondering when faced with our suggestion for a business 'park' which so clearly lacks the balance we had reminded about between town and green space, the park-like quality, in fact. Mediating between building and tree and shrub and building and tree and ... is not our business, not part of the basic architectural structure, and certainly not in a place that in formless juxtaposition, in mere obedience to the constraints of nature, agriculture, industry and residence has indeed become a mere 'estate', and not a place in its own right.

If Gladbeck is going to raise its profile here with a new 'wave of cultivation' under the aegis of IBA, by industrialization of the fourth kind, somewhere between Toyota dealer and eco-tech, then the heritage of industrial culture and industrial buildings that can still be recognized must be exploited for the present purpose in terms of density, format, and dimension.

It was our task to test and correct the competition premises against the actual potential of the 'area': what was wanted was a simple, efficient, planned basic structure involving development, facilities, definition of lots and use – the plans show this. But what was also wanted was of course the image, the Corporate Identity of this piece of Gladbeck, helping the developer to make a successful direct approach, aquiring powerful businesses.

The working models provide the following picture, in my view:
– the tight sequence of the office, laboratory and production buildings growing up on the small plots up to a maximum of 6 storeys in a density that pays in view of the expense contamination has made necessary – a little town, no, not in the town, but 'in the area'. The firm spatial edges of this urban strip, not too low, for all the freedom of interchange with the green and development nodes, are vital for the success of this townscape;
– the site beyond these edges is left over, derelict, has turned into a no-man's-land, partly because it has been poisoned, but above all held in reserve, a reproach: for the development of larger, related green areas, for special use and special buildings, for rounding off industrial building complexes worthy of protection.

So not perpetuation of an estate, not the park (the green areas in the immediate neighbourhood run to hundreds of hectares) – a compact, intelligible, disciplined sequence of buildings with an almost urban structure relate to the architectural heritage of the first, long-gone 'heyday' of the region.

Stituation	site plan

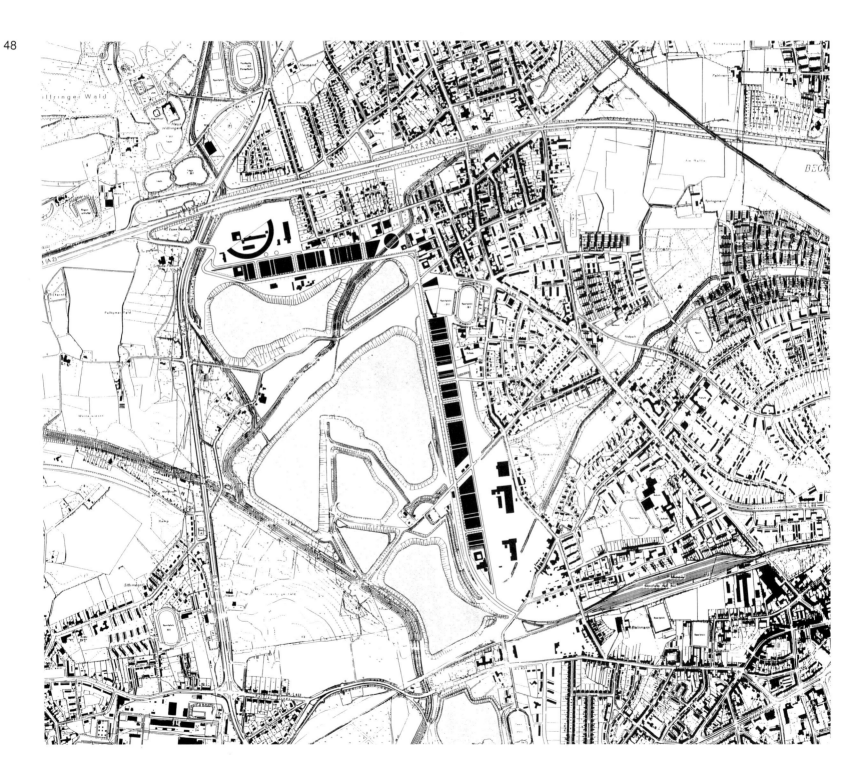

Ansicht von der Haupterschliessung
das Gelände der Zeche Graf-Moltke

view along Main supply line
site plan of Graf-Moltke district

49

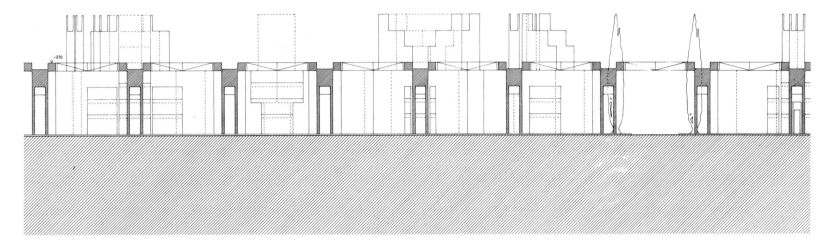

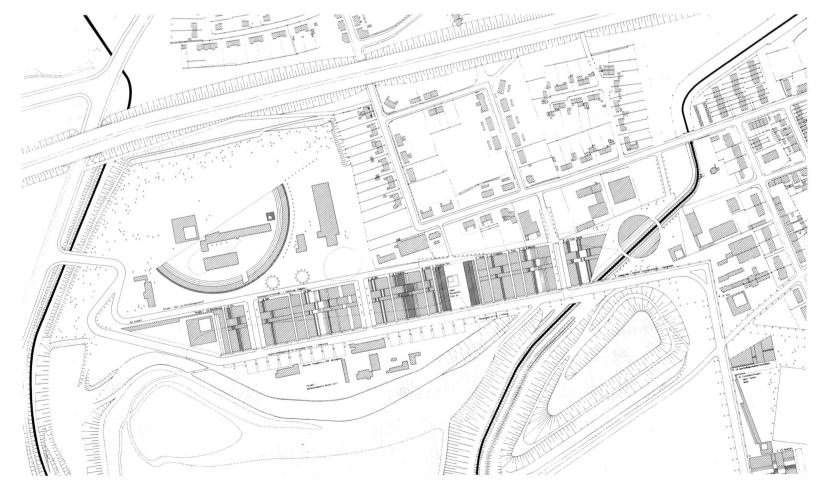

Deutsche Bank Unter den Linden, Berlin

1991, Axel Schultes
in Bangert Jansen Scholz Schultes
mit Charlotte Frank und Christoph Witt

The Deutsche Bank Unter den Linden, Berlin

1991, Axel Schultes
in Bangert Jansen Scholz Schultes
with Charlotte Frank and Christoph Witt

'Das Alte kennen und lieben und es ins Neue hinüberretten' – auch angesichts des wenig anmutigen Hauses Unter den Linden 15 muss sich ein Architekt zur Liebe zwingen können, wenn er denn der Aufgabe gerecht werden will, aus Alt und Neu das Dritte, den Berliner Hauptsitz der Deutschen Bank, in angemessener, moderner Gestalt entstehen zu lassen.

Der Atmosphäre des Hauses, das 1920 schon einen Hauch der späten '30er Jahre' vorwegnahm, ist mit einer blossen Renovierung nicht beizukommen – ein paar chirurgische Eingriffe in das kafaeske Gemäuer tun schon Not, um Licht und Ausblick, Orientierung also und Wohlbefinden im Altbau möglich zu machen; auch um räumliche Grosszügigkeit herzustellen, um trotz der denkmalpflegerisch festgeschriebenen Fassade dem repräsentativen Charakter der Lage und der Nutzungsvorstellung des Bauherrn gerecht zu werden.

Wie wir dabei das Skalpell geführt haben, zeigen die Pläne: die konkreten Planungsprämissen stelle ich hier noch einmal zusammen:
– die Orientierung des Gebäudes zur Behrenstrasse, mit seinem, pardon, Hinterteil zu den Linden, gehört ausgetauscht: mindestens die gesamte Erdgeschosszone, auch die der 13, öffnet sich über die Länge zum Boulevard. Dazu gehört konsequenterweise die Absenkung des Hochparterres auf etwa Linden-Niveau – die gesamte Eingangs- und Kundehalle muss frei und grosszügig, also niveaugleich erschlossen sein.
– die Innenhöfe, auf Traufhöhe 22 m überglast, durch die transparenter hergerichteten Querbauten der 13 und 15 zu *einem* Raum verbunden, sind, zusammen mit den parallel geführten Licht- und Treppenschlitzen, das eigentlich integrierende, zentraliisierende, orientierungstiftende Element des neuen 'Alt'-Baues.
– der Dachaufbau der 15, auch von der Denkmalpflege ungeliebt, ist ein eklatanter Verstoss gegen die strassenräumliche Konvention der Linden – und hat das Lindenstatut mit seiner 22.00 m-Traufregulierung von 1929 provoziert. Mit seiner Höhe von 34.0 m unmittelbar an der Bauflucht und über die volle Länge des Hauses verweigert es jedes harmonische Zusammengehen mit den barocken, auch neobarocken Baudenkmälern des Umfeldes. Es gehört abgetragen.
– an seiner Stelle, eben nicht an seiner Stelle, liesse sich, deutlich zurückgesetzt und mit seiner Rundform jede Traufkanten- und Strassenprofilüberhöhung vermeidend, der gläserne Zylinder als erstes, einziges Neubauelement über dem alten Gemäuer errichten. Innenräumlich schon vom Erdgeschoss ab durch den gesamten Altbau hindurch vorbereitet, nimmt es die Leitungs- und Rekreationsfunktionen des Hauses auf.

In dringend notwendiger Ergänzung einer Altbaufassade, die dem Wunsch der Deutschen Bank auf angemessene Selbstdarstellung sicher nicht gerecht werden kann, kommt diesem Element grosse Bedeutung zu. Als architektonisches Zeichen einer gewichtigen, aber privaten Organisation wahrt es selbstbewusst Distanz zu den öffentlichen Institutionen und Objekten der Dorotheenstadt.

'To know and love the old and save it to become new' – an architect must be able to force himself to love even the less than graceful building at 15 Unter den Linden, if he wants to do justice to the task of turning old and new into a third thing, the Berlin head office of the Deutsche Bank, in an appropriate, modern shape.

The atmosphere of the building, which anticipated a breath of the late 30s even in 1920, cannot be overcome by mere renovation – a few surgical incisions into the kafkaesque walls are definitely necessary to create light and a view, in other words to make a sense of where you are and a bit of comfort possible in the old building; also in order to produce generous spatial scale, to do justice to the prestigious character of the site and the client's ideas for using the building despite the listed façade.

The plans show how we used the scalpel; I'll list the concrete planning premises here:
– the orientation of the building to Behrenstrasse, with its, sorry, backside to Unter den Linden, has to be reverted: at least the whole of the ground floor area, that of number 13 as well, opens on to the boulevard along its full length. Logically this also involves lowering the upper ground floor roughly to the level of Unter den Linden – the whole entrance and banking hall must be free and spacious, in other words accessible on the same level,
– the inner courtyards, glazed at the eaves height of 22 m, combined into a *single* space by the transparent arrangement of the transverse buildings of numbers 13 and 15, are, together with the parallel arrangement of the light and staircase slits, the element that actually integrates, centralizes and gives orientation to the new 'old' building.
– the rooftop structure of number 15, unpopular even with preservation authority, is a flagrant breech of Unter den Linden's street convention, and provoked the Lindenstatute of 1929 with its 22 m eaves regulation. With its height of 34 m directly on the building line and along the full length of the building it refuses to merge harmoniously with the baroque and neobaroque buildings around it. It should be demolished.
– in its place, and precisely not in its place, it was possible to build the glass cylinder, clearly set back and avoiding any excessive raising of eaves edges or street profile because of its circular shape, as the first and only new building element above the old walls. In terms of interior space it is anticipated even from ground floor level through the whole old section, and it accommodates the management and recreation functions needed in the building.

As an urgently necessary complement to an old building façade that can certainly not do justice to the Deutsche Bank's wish for appropriate self-representation, this element acquires considerable significance. As an architectonic symbol of an important but private organization it keeps its self-conscious distance from the public institutions and objects in the Dorotheenstadt.

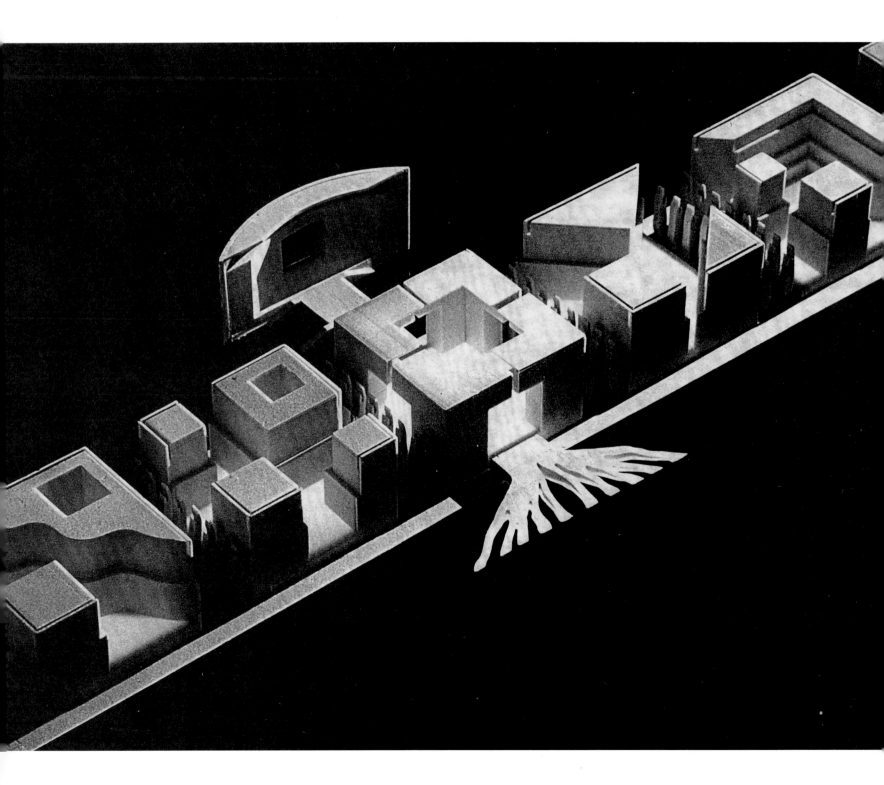

Hemmerichsweg office centre, Frankfurt

1991, Axel Schultes
in Bangert Jansen Scholz Schultes
with Charlotte Frank

A Frankfurt IBA in Hemmerichsweg – perhaps 7 × 7 architects will ultimately be concerned about the urban shape of the seven blocks in the no-mans-land between goods station and exhibition grounds. Seven architects will not define their own limits – there will have to be a 'Hemmerich statute' to show the way open to designs, freedom of planning and planning needs must be sensibly controlled in urban development terms, in other words rigidly laid down in view of the relatively unstructured surrounding area, which itself provides little order; this urban development convention fixes a few things definitely:
– the small plot structure anyway,
– block size of 72 × 72 m (7×),
– building denity of 4.4 on average, related to the building plot,
– development of a general ground floor with a block terrace at + 6 m,
– and material regulations prescribing stone covering for the rectangular surfaces and transparent or metallic material for all façades inside the block.

Crammed in between the secret path to the exhibition grounds in the north and clanking lorries and railway trucks in the south, developing the block platforms 6 m above street level acquires a special significance: making it pleasant to be in the cafés and canteens, for short breaks and at lunchtime, offering air and a bit of a view to complement the world of commerce and shops in the Hemmerichs 'boulevard'.

A front and a back can be read into the situation if you absolutely must – we didn't shy away from providing a centre for this city-strip – with an urban loggia in the middle of the seven blocks, also intended to be square in front of the exhibition grounds, and later as access from the fair to the park; a large hotel should serve this square as a semi-public institution – with shops, restaurants, cafés, espresso bars etc., throughout the hotel foyer on the ground floor up to the 6 m level of the loggia-square area.

Rebuilding the end of the freight hall is vital for the new quarter – having to find your way to this piece of a new city amidst diesel fumes and Euro-pallets would be a bad start for this extensive operation – and so we have reorganized things: the lorries push their way in only from the sides, from north and south, to the 2 × 8 slots in the loading ramp (that will be very easy to organize, even if the railway authorities are sure to be sceptical at first), street and pavements are more released to be urban and normal, and the raised office buildings can be accessible without a lorry blockade.

A pretty rigid city centre block concept for Frankfurt's sense of city? I think that the mixture of investors and architects that is developing here needs a tight corset: colleagues will make things more colourful than the city can take at this point anyway.

Situation	site plan

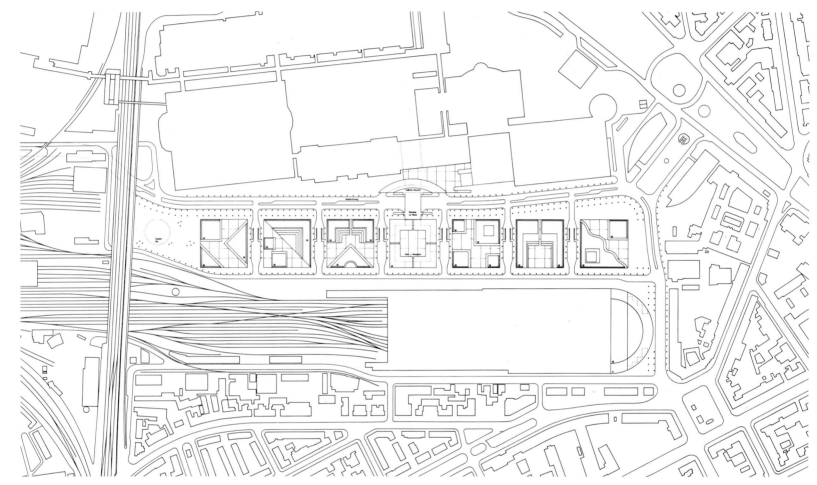

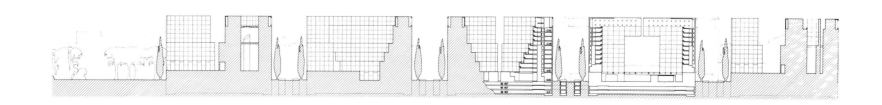

Grundriss Blockterrasse + 6.00 m

block terrace + 6.00 m ground plan

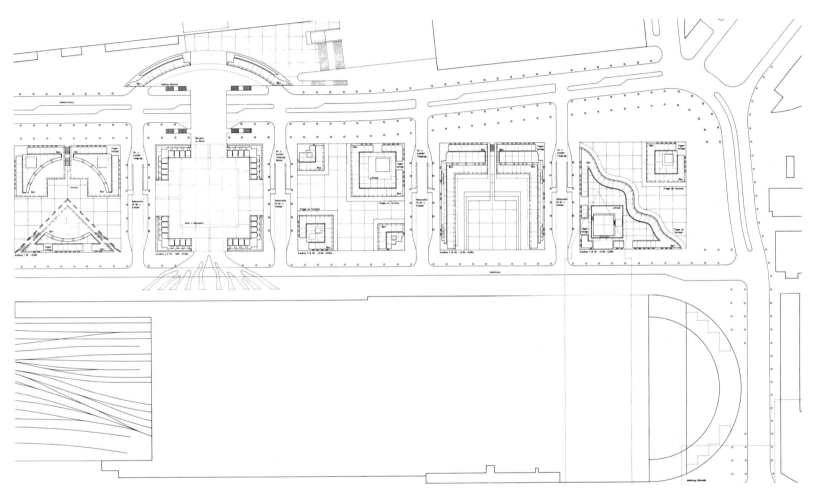

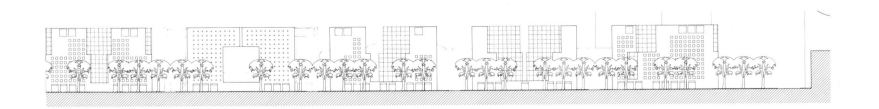

Berlin Friedrichstadt

1991, Axel Schultes
in Bangert Jansen Scholz Schultes
with Charlotte Frank

Rebuilding the three Gendarmenmarkt blocks in the heart of old Berlin, in the context of an international investor-initiated competition, was reason enough for an urban-structural test design to examine urban space conventions in Friedrichstadt, a hundred years old but still relevant, and in places other than Friedrichstadt as well, now that Berlin has different problems, the problems of being a capital city again. The focus of planning intentions here is not so much the fate of the three central Friedrichstrasse blocks as a new, general principle for Berlin blocks and street spaces. There should be speculation here about the elements of a street idea of European calibre, between the culs-de-sac of urban models under discussion at the moment: a building density of 5.0 as a broad inner city planning concensus, combined with the Berlin eaves-height limit of 22 m, leads to constricted filling of usable space, leads to spatial impoverishment of the blocks and to large-scale standardization of use, to squandering the city – abandonment of the block periphery and thus of ordered urban space (to name the counter-model) combined with generous high-rise development is – still – forbidden to us by our European-sentimental instinct.

So this suggestion pursues a third possibility: releasing the block mass from the traditional city base of the Berlin eaves, up on to a second urban plane, to an upper city with a height limit of e.g. 44 m, retaining the 5.0 density, of course. The advantages of a new convention of this kind are obvious:
– the block would then be more finely structured, more 'spatial', and able to compensate for the inevitable loss of traditional plot organization, making it possible to plan mixed use again;
– sensible, urban, not to say metropolitan stratification of use, perceptible in the higher, double street- and cityscape, can be pushed ahead, and could even embrace the problem of inner-city living;
– the spatial quality of the city base will then be porous, and can at last, complement the streets and squares and open up the private seclusion of the traditional block, transform it into a third kind of public, urban space;
– the spatial arrangement of the city, the sense in which it can be perceived, is preserved, open to planning, and comprehensible within a new, obligatory urban development maxim, a new 'Berlin statute'.

Situation um den Gendarmenmarkt
Grundriss Basement

site plan
basement ground plan

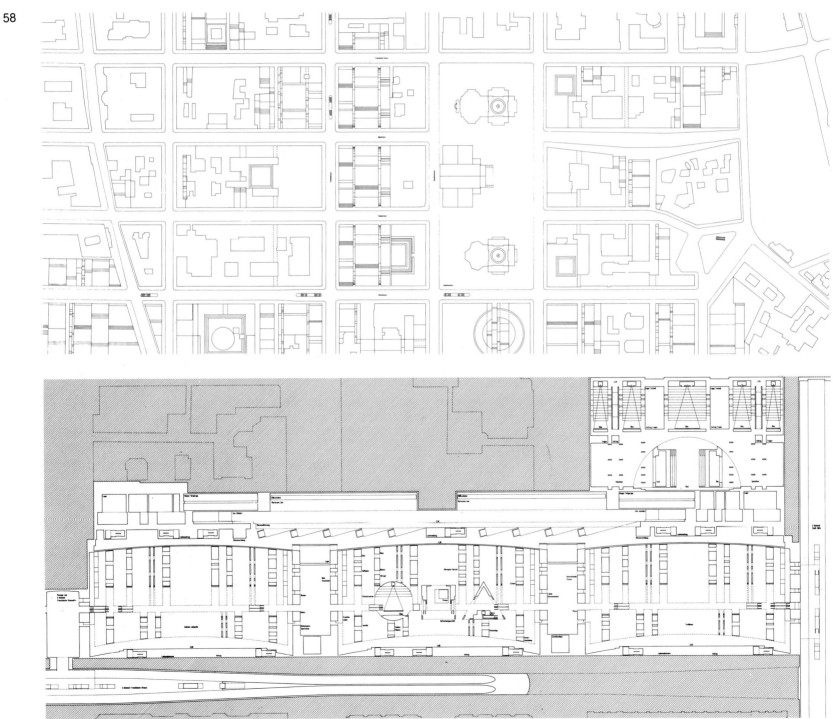

Blick nach Osten über Friedrichstrasse und Gendarmenmarkt

view east accross Friedrichstrasse and Gendarmenmarkt

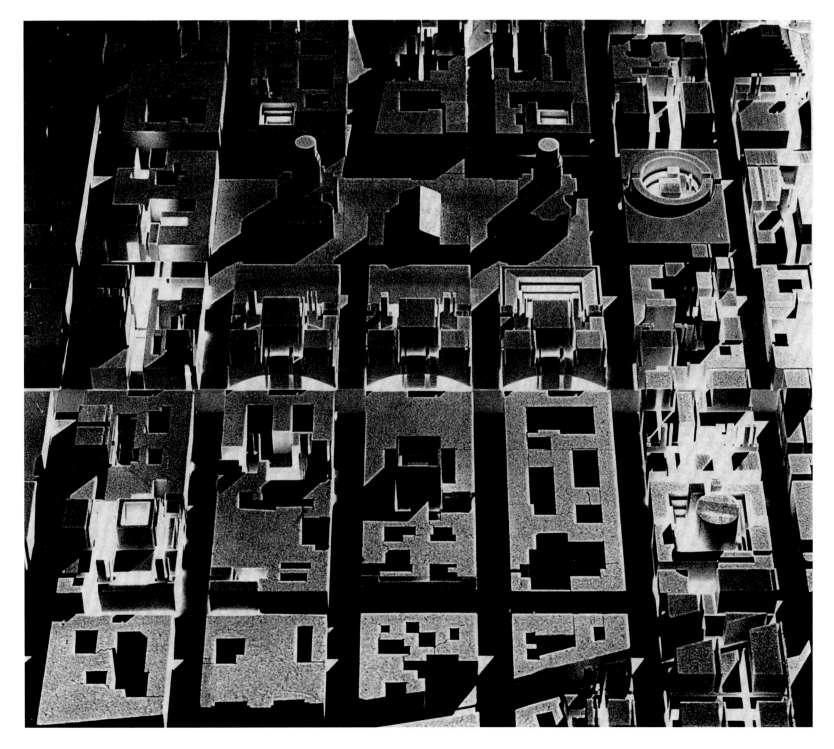

Schnitt parallel zur Friedrichstrasse
Grundriss Erdgeschoss

cross-section parallel to Friedrichstrasse
ground floor ground plan

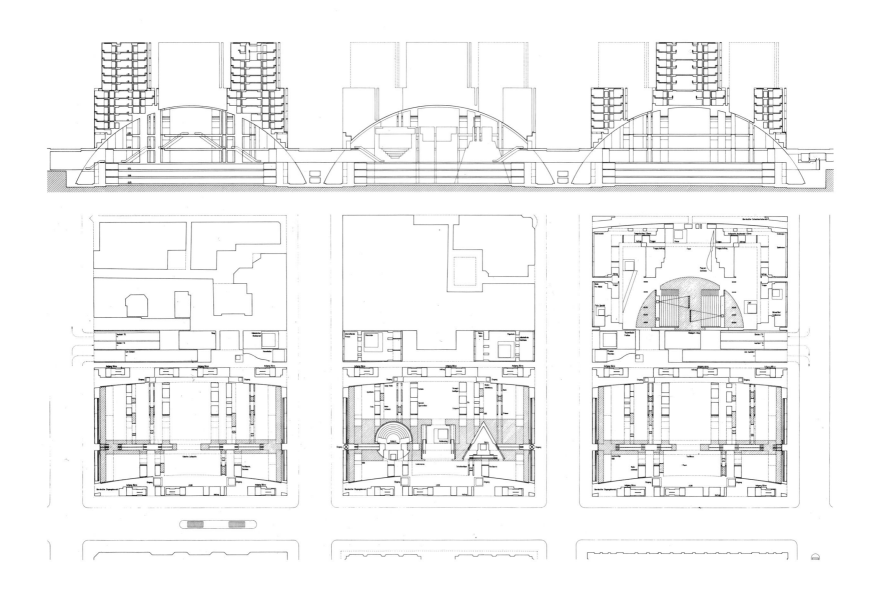

Blick nach Osten, bei Nacht — Friedrichstrasse in Bildmitte   view east, at night — Friedrichstrasse in the center

Schnitt durch den südlichen Block
Schnitt durch den nördlichen Block
Grundriss Obergeschosse

cross-section through southern block
cross-section through nothern block
upper floors ground plan

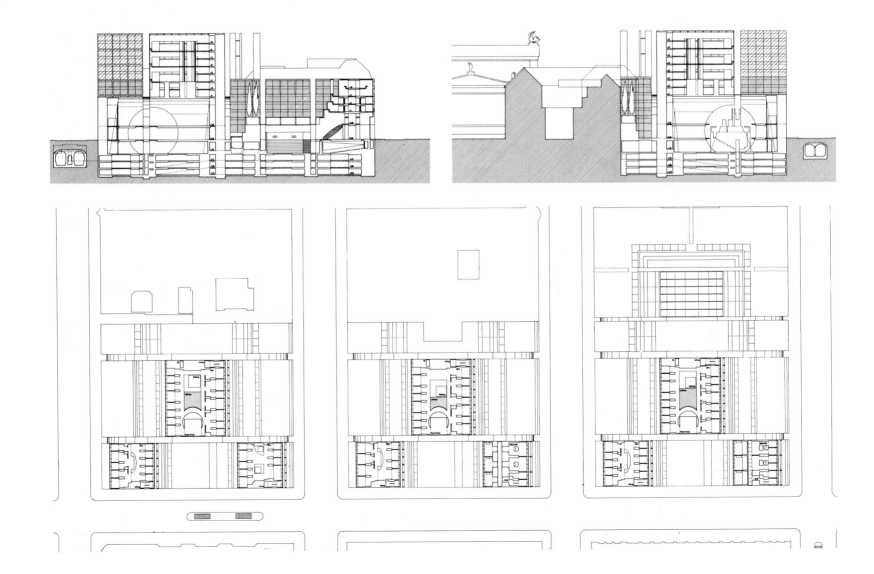

die interne Plaza – 'Mutterhöhle des Konsums'   the interior plaza – 'the mothercave of consuming'

Dresden Altmarkt

1991, Axel Schultes
in Bangert Jansen Scholz Schultes
with Charlotte Frank

Neither the 'whispering invocation ot the imperfect' in manner of Leon Krier for instance, nor the finally free market desire to invest in the singular object without an urban concept will help Dresden back in its spaces, give back to the heart of Dresden a meaningful, dense, rhythmically organized network of streets and squares.

Only courage and enough time for a general reformulation of the structure of the urban space can prevent a third destruction of Dresden. Wanting 'Dresden as a work of art', but producing Dresden as a patchwork of pieces in a great rush on a few choiced lots: working against this is the primary task as well and in particularly here in the Altmarkt report.

It is not possible to proceed in this 'without some delusions': the shape of Dresden, the master plan at least for the 400 m radius of the heart of the town cannot be drawn up in a hurry; but a picture must be formed, helpfully on model photos, in defiance of the carnival night of February 13th, a planning intention must be formulated, spatial order must be found. Public space, available by the hectare as a derelict city centre area, must be transformed into controlled public space. And the models for this are not to be found, as dealings at the last workshop suggested, in some European metropolis or other – the town's own architectural tradition, the spirit of order and musical temperament of the Zwinger in particular must be translated into new spaces and new architecture, must help to affirm the identity of the city.

Not neoclassical or postmodern mentality of style and good taste (one has only to think of Schinkel's ignorant verdict on Pöppelmann), only spatial, rhythmic instinct, the courageous 'tastelessness' of baroque can be the starting point for new planning. Dresden would be ill-advised to administer this heritage merely as a monument.

'Re'building always seems to be a mistake: thus Julius Posener in Potsdam, on the same problem. Building the Altmarkt up again in sensible proportions – that could come off well with luck – creates all the more problems in the immediate vicinity. For us the Altmarkt extends from Prager Strasse in the south to the Johanneum in the north as a sequence of space protected by overhanging roofs, rather like a galeria thus, the central urban element in Dresden between the main station and the new town; it is to be hoped not dissimilar in attractiveness as an area to stroll around to the Ramblas in Barcelona; the semicircle of ring boulevard between the Pirnaischer Platz and Postplatz attemps to connect the islands of blocks of the south old town into an urban structure (the boulevard carries all the traffic around the old town, ideally 5,000 to 10,000 parking spaces should be built underneath it). Ernst-Thälmann-Strasse, as an alternative to the always thinkable dense row of trees, could easily be transformed into a sequence of squares of variable dimensions; the suggestion for the Neumarkt will cause some furrowed brows in the town: the old outline of the Neumarkt, an urban curiosity, should that of all things be restored?; the gigantic, desolate Webergasse block should pick up the old, finely-structured street pattern in passage form.

Modell – nördlicher Teil des neuen 'Altmarkts'
Konzept Skizze, Konzeptplan

model – northern part of the new 'Altmarkt'
concept, sketch, concept plan

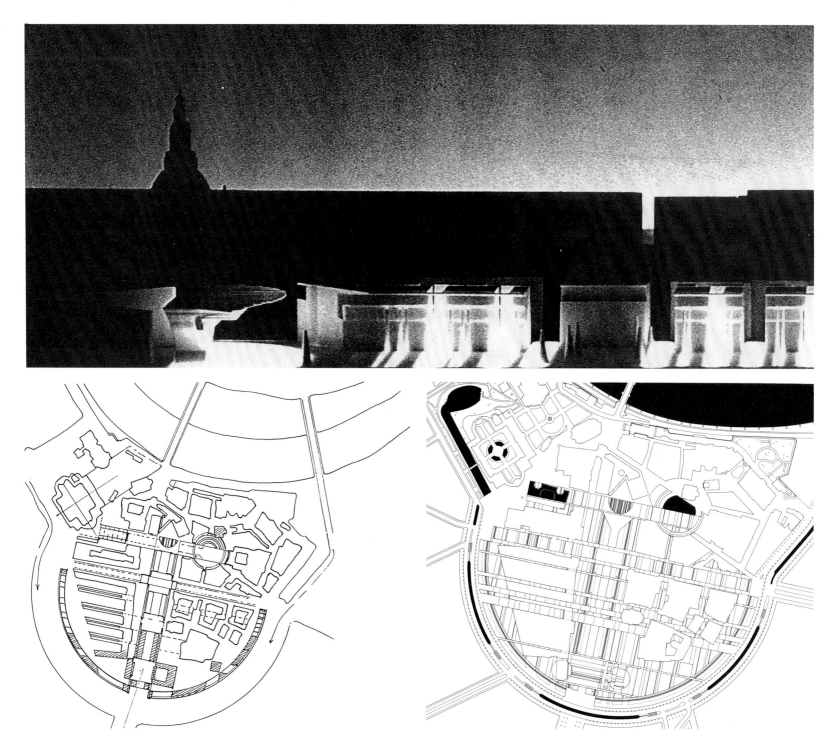

Modell – südlicher Teil des neuen 'Altmarkts'
Grundrissausschnitt Basement
Grundrissausschnitt Erdgeschoss

model – southern part of the new 'Altmarkt'
basement ground plan
ground floor ground plan

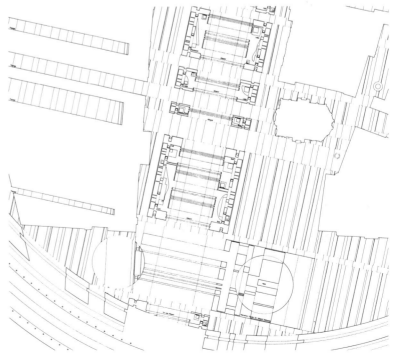

Blick über die Frauenkirche zum 'Altmarkt'
Teil des 'Altmarkt'-Profils vor der Kreuzkirche

view accross Frauenkirche to the 'Altmarkt'
part of the 'Altmarkt' profile in front of the Kreuzkirche

nördliches Altmarktende am Johanneum
nördliches Altmarktende mit dem 'Quercus Saxonicus'

nothern end of the 'Altmarkt' at the Johanneum
nothern end of the 'Altmarkt' with the 'Quercus Saxonicus'

Una porta per Venezia

1990, Axel Schultes
in Bangert Jansen Scholz Schultes
mit Charlotte Frank

Viele Wege führen nach Rom, nur ein einziger nach Venedig. Die Via Appia zum Beispiel treppt am Ziel ihres Weges römisch-vornehm in den Hafen von Brindisi, die A4, die Autostrada della Serenissima, verendet kläglich in den Dieselwolken der Piazza Roma. Fünfzig Autobusse zur gleichen Zeit am gleichen Ort (so die Forderung des Auslobers) lassen sich ohne Schaden für das Entree Venedigs nicht zwischen die Bäume mogeln – sie müssen unters Pflaster der neuen Piazza oder sie fahren nur vor, sind abgestellt auf einer der neuen Inseln fürs mobile Blech (das wäre leicht zu bewerkstelligen, ist aber nicht Aufgabe hier im Wettbewerb).

Sind die Busse erst einmal untergebracht, unter dem neuen Platz, lässt sich dieses Stadtfoyer entwickeln: exakt auf der Nahtstelle zwischen dem Vor-Ort, der Stadt der isolierten Objekte, und dem alten Venedig, der Stadt der Räume, der Plätze, Gassen und Kanäle, formuliert die neue Piazzale Roma Ende und Grenze von Lärm und Gift des Draussen, den Beginn althergebrachter Urbanität. Das Doppelte dieser Stadt aus Wasser und Land, die Komplexität ihrer Organe ist auch Ausgangspunkt für das baulichte Konzept der Piazzale Roma:

weniger ein Fragment, eher eine Subtraktion, ein Rest, eine Erinnerung – die Hälfte eines Gebäudeblockes, die Hälfte eines Platzraumes, die Hälfte eines Parks – also Platz und Haus in einem, Objekt und Raum zugleich.

Die Öffnung dieses merkwürdigen Torraumes zu den drei Brücken über den Rio Nuovo ist der Schlüssel, mit dem Venedig sich dem Besucher, und dem Bewohner, aufschliesst, die Wege freigibt zum Zattere, zum Rialto, den Canal Grande entlang.

Eine 'Architettura della Citta', das sozusagen Normale von Wänden, Dachplatten, grossen und kleinen Öffnungen und Schlitzen, gibt die Substanz für das Platzgebäude – die eigentliche Porta da Venezia aber, die Schwelle zwischen drinnen und draussen, ist mit den Mitteln unserer 'Architettura rationale' kaum zu gestalten; zu bilderleer, zu anonym, zu kalt käme eine solche Latinita daher. Venedig, künstlicher, gefährdeter, orientalischer als alle ihre römisch-italischen Schwestern byzantinischer, heiterer, bei aller gebotenen Modernität, versteht sich: die Grosse Eiche, Fundament der Stadt (und der Flotte, damals) in blau-grün oxydiertem Stahlblech, lieber noch in Stein, dem stahlarmierten, heisst die Besucher willkommen nach ihrer Fahrt über die Lagune.

Fünfzig Busse unter Niveau zu legen ist kein geringer Aufwand, aber machbar: wir haben das konstruktiv und statisch untersucht. Der Busbahnhof, 2,5 m unter Wasserspiegel, ist dabei alles andere als ein Keller – der Steinbelag der Piazza wird unterbrochen durch Streifen begehbarer, befahrbarer Glasflächen, die das Aufsuchen der Busse bei Tageslicht möglich machen. Das wandartig-mehrstöckige Gebäude darüber beherbergt alle Nutzungen, die das Programm fordert und die die Stadt an einem solchen Ort für wünschenswert hält: Cafébars und Hotelreservation, Ticketstation und Wartehallen, Stadtinformation und Touristenpolizei, Ausstellungsräume der Stadt und der Biennale, etc. ...

A Gateway for Venice

1990, Axel Schultes
in Bangert Jansen Scholz Schultes
with Charlotte Frank

Many roads lead to Rome but only one to Venice. For example, on reaching its destination the Via Appia descends in grand Roman style to Brindisi harbour; the A4, the Autostrada della Serenissima, comes to a piteous halt disappearing into the exhaust fumes of the Piazza Roma. It is simply not possible to find space for fifty buses all at once (Promoter's stipulation) between the trees without impinging on the gateway to Venice – the only solution is to put them underground, beneath the new piazza, or to send them further on where they can park on one of the new islands for tin cans on wheels (this could easily be arranged, but it's not what the competition is about).

With the buses safely disposed of beneath the new square we can get on with the developement of this foyer to the city: located at the point where the hinterland city of isolated objects meets the old Venice of squares, alleyways and canals, the new Piazzale Roma marks the end of the noise and dirt outside and the beginning of traditional urban life. The duality of this city of water and land, the complexity of its organs, also provide the basis for this architectural concept for the Piazzale Roma:

less a fragment than a subtraction, a remainder, a reminder – half a built block, half a square, half a park – in other words square and building in one object and space.

The opening of this strange gateway to the three bridges over the Rio Nuovo is the key with which Venice opens itself to its visitors and inhabitants, paving the way to the Zattere, to the Rialto, and along the Canal Grande.

The substance of the building is provided by an 'Architettura della Citta', the 'normal' architecture of walls, roof slabs, large and small openings and slits – however, the actual Porta da Venezia, the threshold marking inside and outside, can hardly rely on the sole means of our 'Architettura rationale; such latinity would be too bare, too anonymous, too cold. Even in its modernity, Venice, more artificial, threatened, oriental than its Italian-Roman sisters dares to present itself differently, in a more Byzantine manner, more serenely: the great Oak, foundation of the city (and formerly of the fleet) in blue-green oxidised steel, better still in concrete, welcomes visitors after their journey across the lagoon.

Putting fifty buses below ground level is no easy task but it can be done: we have undertaken a constructional and structural analysis. The bus station, 2.5 m below sea level is anything but a cellar – the stone tiling of the piazza is interspersed with strips of glass which can be walked and driven on and which provide daylight for the bus passengers. All the facilities stipulated in the programme, and which the city deems necessary in such a place, can be found in the wall-like, multi-storey building above: coffee bars and hotel reservation offices, ticket offices and waiting rooms, city information point, tourist police, exhibition rooms for the Biennale etc. ...

Massenmodell – Canal Grande am oberen Bildrand   full model – Canal Grande at the upper edge

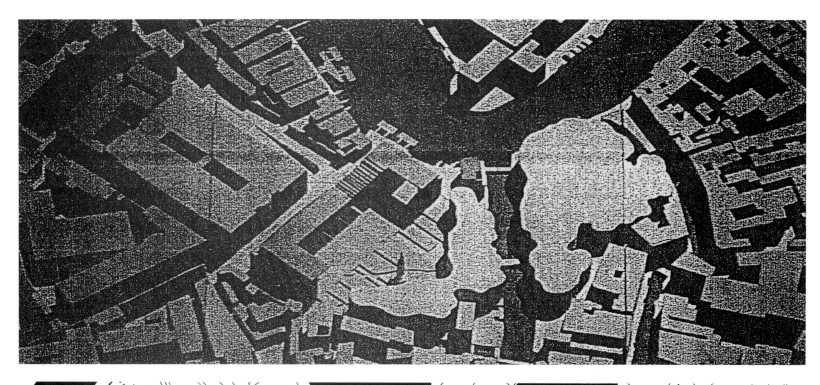

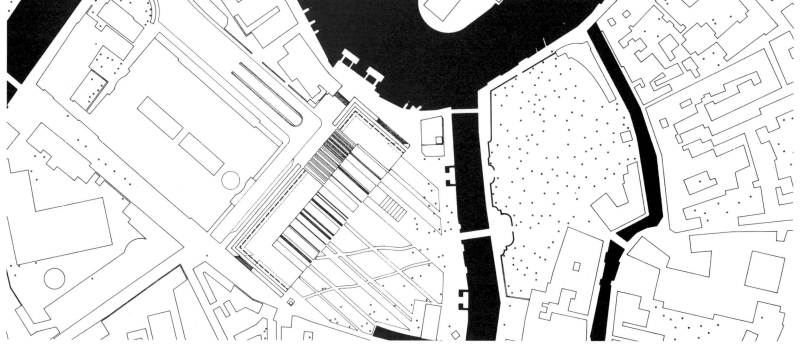

die Piazzale Roma bei Nacht	Piazzale Roma at night
Grundriss Basement – Busbahnhof	basement ground plan – busstation
Grundiss Erdgeschoss	ground floor ground plan

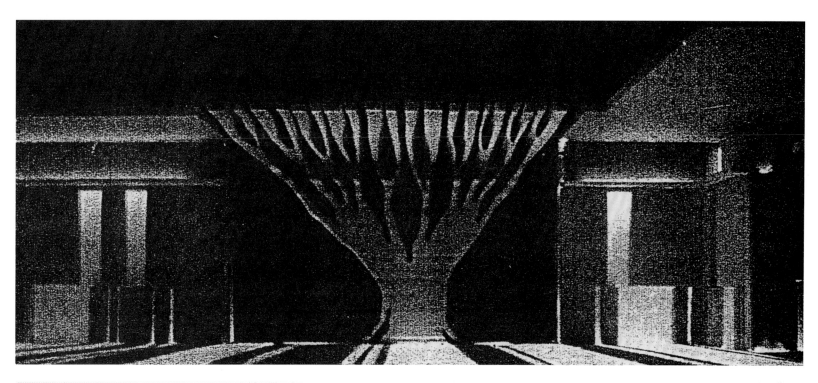

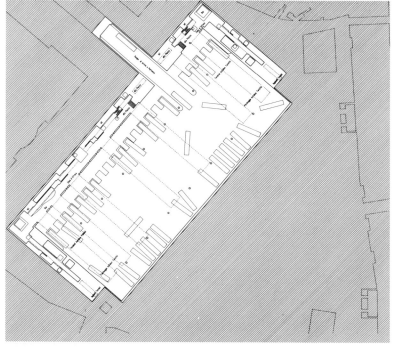

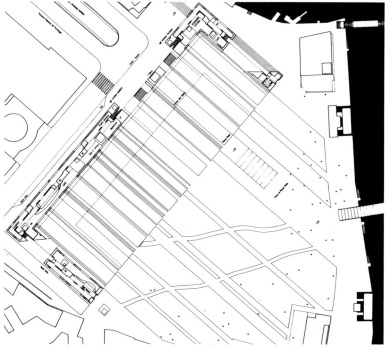

Extension to Witten Town Hall

1990, Axel Schultes
in Bangert Jansen Scholz Schultes

This planning approach, the fourth in the meantime, is also a servant of two masters: the demand for a building that is open and welcoming to townspeople seeking advice, but also for a structure in Witten's central square that is again pleasant and usable. The previous 1987 design has also been once more thoroughly revised, simplified, tightened up, straightened and put to rights with an eye on the not exactly bulging city coffers:
– the Grand Staircase gives access to the entire new building, and with its foyer areas and attached galleries gives an 'a priori' orientation, without asking, for all offices, meetings, departments;
– there are more than enough corridors, and kafkaesque counting of doors around three corners, in the old building. The new building gives access to each office via the hall galleries, with natural light in every square metre of the building. The model section shows the complete new building: the hall façade with the office space galleries, the staircase with its foyers and waiting areas, two large meeting rooms hung in the hall space, above the garage spindle are placed the citizens' office and the council chamber with its visitors' galleries – this council chamber takes itself seriously – the town council requires appropriate spaces for concentrated work, discussions and decisions – not only the citizens' office and the rent rebate office, it too is a 'public affair'.
– the new main entrance, roofed in the cut-open profile of the building, with a square in front of it leading to Bahnhofstrasse is an introduction to the Grand Staircase – the connection to the old building via terrace, bridge or roof is being further examined;
– the 'town terrace', continuing the new building by other means, (still) takes the tram tracks into account on its southern edge. Town hall square and town terrace are considered in the previous design in principle in their topographical development, but not yet as equipped with artistic, horticultural, informative and technical elements.

The fundamental improvement of the quality of the interior space, ease in finding one's way around, the structural clarity of the new revised design is obvious – a design development in this direction was only possible through a more rigorous basic approach, moving the newly building project more expressly to the centre of the structural planning intentions: developing architectural expression not only from the conditions of the place and within the framework of the programme, as it were continuing to write it, but adding old to new, bringing them into confrontation, according to situation and opportunity, more independently and certainly less comfortably. Obvious town shape needs not only interpretative sensibility, but imagination directed at the new. Simply continuing the sequence of rooms and roofs in the town hall on all sides, certainly a convenient design solution, was the decisive obstacle to the development of a sensible concept for a town hall that would encourage communication, and be generous and neightbourly.

Massenmodel full model
Grundriss 1.Obergeschoss 1st floor ground plan

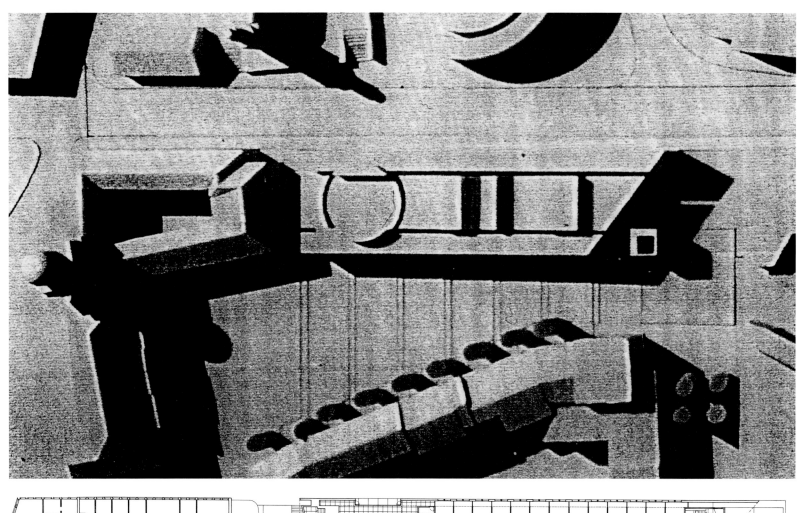

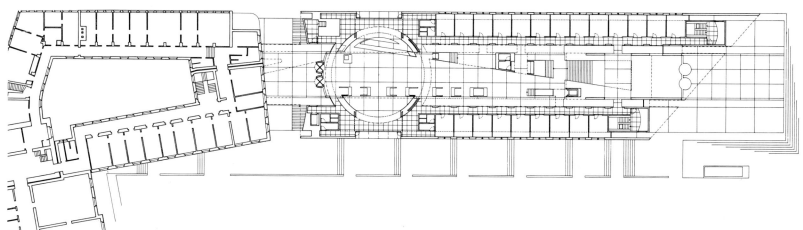

Schnittmodel
Grundriss 4.Obergeschoss

model cross-section
4th floor ground plan

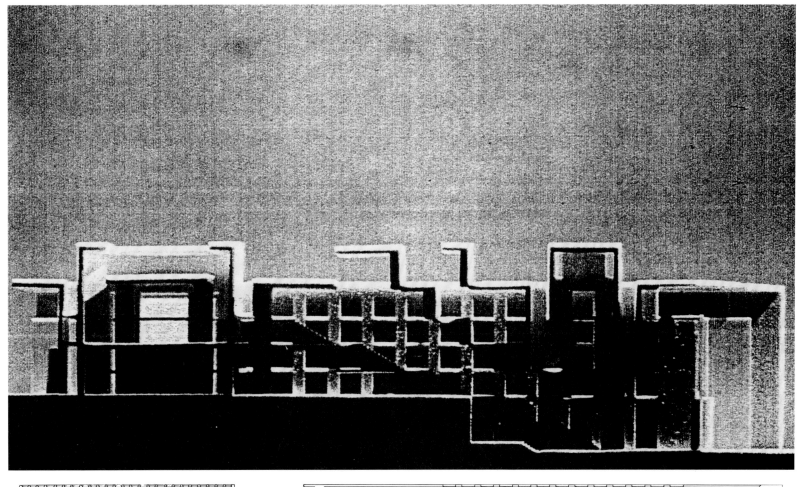
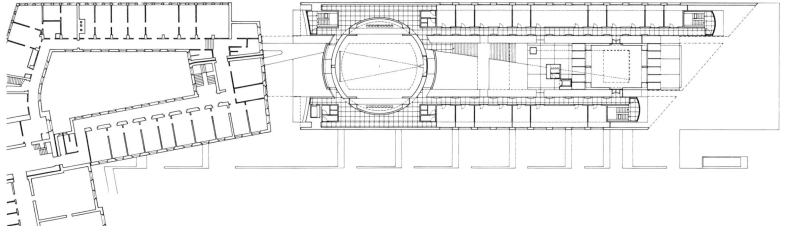

Dachaufbau Lützowplatz 7, Berlin

1990, Axel Schultes
in Bangert Jansen Scholz Schultes

New roof at 7 Lützowplatz, Berlin

1990, Axel Schultes
in Bangert Jansen Scholz Schultes

Ein Dach abreissen, um ein neues zu bauen; sich häuslich einrichten mit Rücksicht auf ein schmales Architektenbudget: gerade und seriell so gut es geht, Holzbinder über zwei Mittelwänden auskragend, extradicke Schrankwände für Küche, Klo und Bad an den massiven Giebeln, Morgen- und Abendsonne auf oder durch die Jalousettenwände und durch die Zwillingsträger in die Tiefe der drei Raumpartien: frisch wohnen müsste sich's da schon lassen, die Winter sind ja nicht mehr, was sie mal waren, und am Ende ist's ein Architektenatelier, weil sich's nicht anders rechnet. (Der Vorgänger dieser spartanischen Planung war eine opulentere Dreierkomposition von Pyramide, Tonne und Doppelgiebel, angedeutet auf S. 133)

Taking off a roof build a new one; making a comfortable home for oneself on a tight architect's budget: as straightforward and mass-produced as possible. Wooden truss beams cantilevered out over two middle walls, extra-sturdy units for kitchen, toilet and bathroom mounted on the solid end walls, morning or evening sun shining on or through the venetian blinds and through the twin beams deep into the three parts of the room: it must be possible to relish living here, anyway the winters aren't what they were, and when all's said and done it's an architect's studio, it's the only way he could afford. (The forerunner of this spartan plan was a more opulent trio composition of pyramid, barrel and double gable, descirbed briefly on page 133.)

Expo '92 Sevilla

1990, Axel Schultes
in Bangert Jansen Scholz Schultes
mit Charlotte Frank, Joachim Koob

Ein Blick die Europäische Avenida hinauf zur ausgerechnet aztekischen Pyramide des spanischen Pavillons könnte das eigentliche Thema dieser Expo erhellen: 'das Zeitalter der Entdeckungen – die Kehrseite der Medaille'. Was europäische Entdeckerwut aus diesem Planeten gemacht hat, soll sich ja mittlerweile herumgesprochen haben – inmitten der expo-offiziellen Blauäugigkeit sollten die Besucher einen Blick riskieren auf den tatsächlichen Zustand dieser Welt, und weltbürgerlich-undeutsch kam das Deutsche immer noch und jahrhundertelang am besten mit sich ins reine. Sollen IBM und Siemens zur Rechten und zur Linken auftragsgemäss in Optimismus machen – der Bundesrepublik stände eine Stunde Ungeschminktes sehr gut zu Gesicht: eine Lust, aus dem riesigen Fundus von 500 Jahren deutscher Nachdenklichkeit eine Ausstellung zu den Überlebenschancen dieses Globus zu machen.

"die Erde ward verdorben, die Wälder sind gestorben, die Städte standen auf":
– 1775 beginnt Matthias Claudius mit der jetzt immer schmerzlicher werdenden Trauerarbeit zur Ermordung unseres Planeten. 'Dieses Thema', so die Auslobung zum ökonomisch-ökologischen Komplex, 'nicht aufdringlich, sondern heiter und bejahend abarbeiten, würde dem Besucher Hoffnung auf seine persönliche Zukunft geben': ?? die armen Architekten haben richtig gelesen? Nein, im Ernst, den Expo-Beitrag in Marlboro-Country anzusiedeln mag versuchen wer will. Zur Sache kommen ist die einzige Rechtfertigung einer solchen Wegwerf-Veranstaltung, etwas mitteilen wollen ohne Besserwissen der einzige Sinn. Hat Greenpeace schon einen Stand auf der Expo? Verläuft sich 'Le Waldsterben' so schlecht? Ein paar Katalysator-Statistiken, ein paar Schwefelfilter – wir haben alles im Griff. Keine Zähne im Mund, aber pfeifen in der Kirche – man darf gespannt sein, was die Bundesrepublik daraus macht.

Architektur am Inhalt entwickeln, Flagge zeigen in Spanien, Spanisches mit hineinnehmen, Reverenz erweisen, ohne sich anzubiedern:
die geschundene Weltesche, Yggdrasil mit der Wolke in der Plaza de Toros – wenn's nicht die Expo wär', würd' ich's mich nicht trauen; die Mezquita von Cordoba, die Unvermeidliche, unter das Wasser von Al Andaluz setzen mit aller wasserdichten deutschen Akribie; ein bisschen Stadtraum einpassen für ein halbes Jahr: die Verwaltung schön bieder zur Briten-Kiste, die einstürzenden Neubauten zum Siemens-Klops; den Rundgang mit einem Rambla-Vergnügen anfangen und ausklingen lassen in den Restaurants, Cafés und Bars auf der Plaza und auf den hängenden Gärten drumherum; die Ausstellung leger auf der grossen Fläche darunter inszenieren, dann etwas schwindelig über die Rolltreppe oben durch die Türme mit den Spezialitäten, Dias vor allem im Schacht des kleinen Turms, Kunst auf der Decke des Vortragssaales, Verschnaufen auf dem Plaza-Dach und an den Restaurants vorbei zurück zur Plaza; auch abkürzen muss man können, unten aus der 'Moschee', aus dem 'Wald', hoch zurück ins Foyer.

Expo '92 Sevilla

1990, Axel Schultes
in Bangert Jansen Scholz Schultes
with Charlotte Frank, Joachim Koob

A glance up the European Avenue to the – of all things – Aztec pyramid of the Spanish pavilion could cast light on actual subject of this exhibition: 'the age of exploration – the other side of the coin'. They say what European exploration mania made of this planet has got about by now – in the midst of all the official exhibition blue-eyed wonderment visitors are to risk taking a look at the way the world actually is – and in a cosmopolitan, un-German sort of way Germanness still can be straight with itself about things, as it has been for centuries. IBM and Siemens should do it, on the right and on the left optimistic as ever – an hour without make-up would suit Germany very well: it would be a pleasure to make an exhibition about the survival chances of this globe from the stock of 500 hundred years of German contemplation.

"die Erde ward verdorben, die Wälder sind gestorben, die Städte standen auf" ("the earth was devastated, the forests had died, the cities stood up"):
– Matthias Claudius began the now even stronger morning about the murder of our planet in 1775. 'It would give the visitor hope about his personal future', said the brief for the economic-ecological complex, 'if this subject were treated cheerfully and affirmatively, rather than stridently': ?? have the poor architects read that correctly? No seriously, anyone who likes can try locating his Expo submission in Marlboro-Country. Getting to the point is the only justification for throw-away events like this, wanting to put something over without being know-all is the only thing that makes sense. Has Greenpeace got a stand at Expo? Is 'Le Waldsterben' selling so badly? A few catalytic converter statistics, a few sulphur filters – we've got it all in hand. "No teeth in his mouth but whistling in the church" – it will be interesting to see what Germany makes of it.

Let architecture grow out of content, show the flag in Spain, include something a bit Spanish, make references without currying favour:
the World Ash Tree stripped, Yggdrasil with the Cloud, in the Plaza de Toros – if it weren't the Expo I wouldn't dare; the Mezquita in Cordoba, the inevitable, put it under the waters of Al Andaluz with fully waterproof German meticulousness; fit in a bit of urban space for six months: the offices nice and neat to go with the British glass box, collapsing pop palaces to face the Siemens dumpling; start the walk round with Rambla delights and let it run gently down in restaurants, cafés and bars in the Plaza and the hanging gardens round about; stage the exhibition informally in the great area underneath, then a bit dizzily, up the escalator and through the towers, with the specialities (slides particularly) in the shaft of the little tower, art on the ceiling of the lecture room, have a breather on the Plaza roof, then past the restaurants back to the Plaza; it must be possible to cut it short, out of the 'mosque' and out of the 'wood' downstairs, back up top, into the foyer.

Massenmodell (rechts angeschnitten der britische Pavillon)
das Wasserbecken als Lichtfilter
Grundriss Ausstellungsgeschoss

full model (British pavilion on the right in cross-section)
the pool as light filter
ground plan of exhibition floor

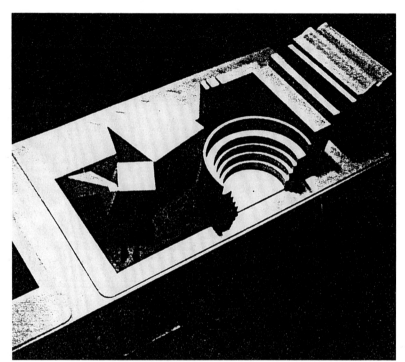

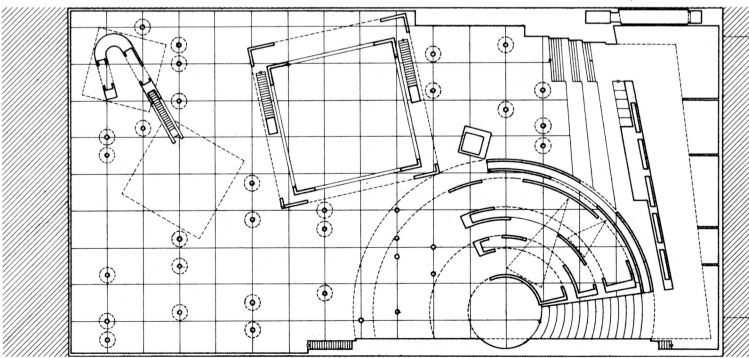

Blick auf die Eingangsrotunde
Grundriss Erdgeschoss

view of the entrance rotunda
ground floor ground plan

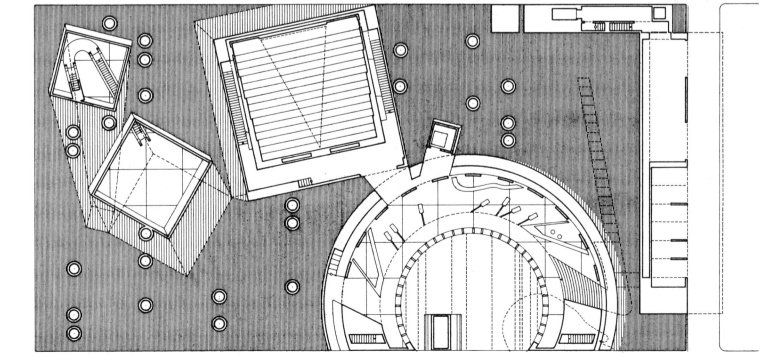

die Ausstellung

the exhibition

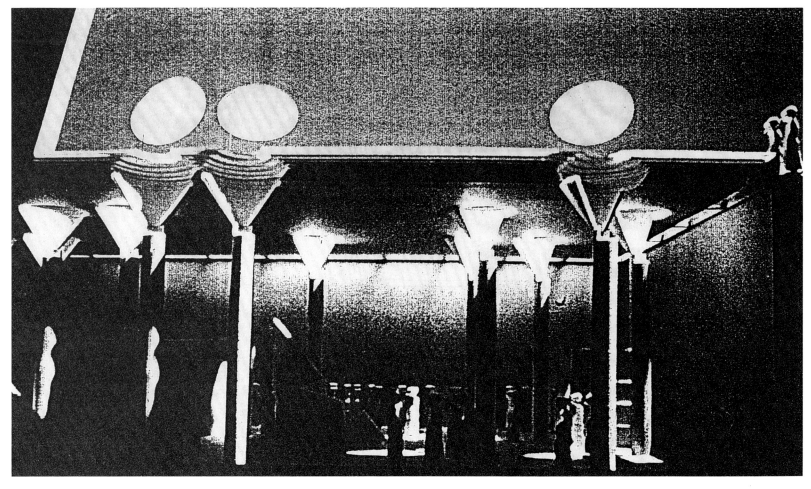

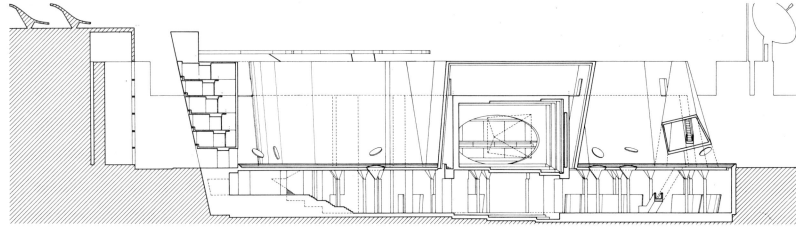

die Ausstellung   the exhibition

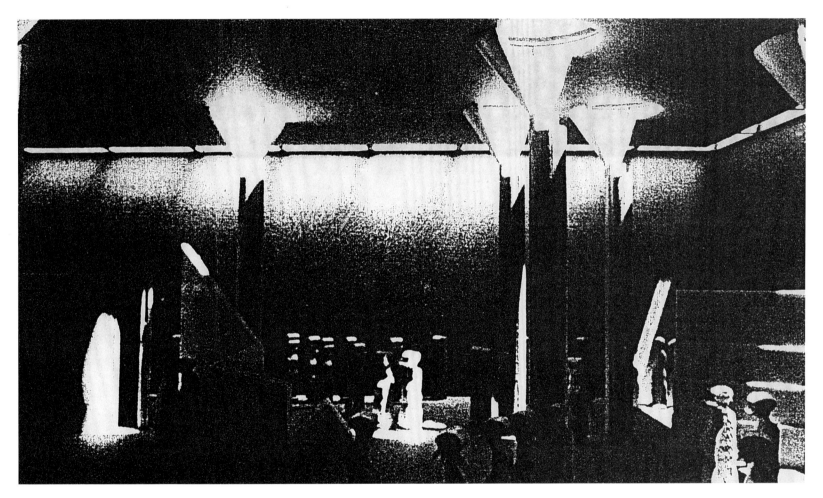

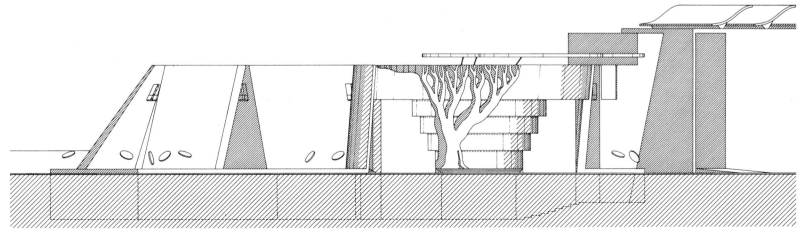

Haus der Geschichte, Stuttgart

1990, Axel Schultes
in Bangert Jansen Scholz Schultes
mit Charlotte Frank

Eher Restfläche als Garten, eher Gegend als Ort – bin selten mit einem ja leicht überschaubaren Bauvolumen so in der Gegend herumgerutscht wie hier hinter dem alten Neuen Schloss und im Vorfeld der schottisch-ägyptischen Moderne. Nicht Schloss und Staatstheater machen Umstände, der Landtag legt sich quer zu allen Konzepten, die das Alte und das ganz Neue im Akademiegarten zusammenfügen wollen. Das Haus der Geschichte als Treppe über der Konrad-Adenauer-Strassenschlucht, in der Schlossachse, am Ende zu ängstlich um Ordnung bemüht? Mauerwinkel, Pavillon oder Rotunden-Ehrgeiz in den Charlottenplatz-Zwickel klemmen und damit am Ende das Übel mehren? Das zweite Klavier, das Pendant zum Landtag, bei aller Liebe zum barocken Ordnungswillen, lässt sich nicht plazieren, die Planie ist dagegen. Schön wär's, von den vielen Irrtümern zur Wahrheit zu reisen – nein, eher ein moderner Kannitverstan, der traditionellen Stadtraum beschreiben will, da, wo keiner ist.

Also flache Räume machen, in Schichtungen arbeiten, die parallel zur Schlossfront schon immer da waren, topographisch: der Nesenbach, die alte Strasse nach Cannstatt, die Hangkante. Das Stirlingsche Rampenspiel sollte für die ganze Hangkante bis zum Staatsarchiv durchgehalten werden, die Doppelreihe der Bäume dazu. Der Zumutung der Blech-Lawine stellt sich der Platanenhain in den Weg, ergänzt um zwei weitere Baumreihen bei Überdeckelung der Bundesstrasse, wenn denn das Symposion von 1987 gegen eine Randbebauung recht behalten soll.

Mit der nächsten Schicht zum Schloss kommt der sogenannte Garten zur Sache: Landtag und Haus der Geschichte sind Teile des dominierenden Grün- und Wasserflächenbandes zwischen Staatstheater und Planie – Geschicke und Geschichte des Landes werden hier gemacht und dort interpretiert. Eine Promenade vom Karlsplatz an Schloss und Staatsheater vorbei, als Gegenstück zum Platanenhain, bestimmt den Übergang in den eigentlichen Schlosspark.

"In unserem Weinberg liegt ein Schatz!"
"An welchem Platz?" schrie alles gleich den Vater an.
"Grabt nur!" O weh, da starb der Mann.

Die Geschichte als Weinberg – eine gut schwäbische Art, den spröden Stoff mit entsprechend räumlicher Illumination ans Publikum zu bringen. Die Stufen und Schichten innen, der geneigte Interpret mag's so sehen wollen, erinnern an den Aufbau des Gartens draussen. Die Modellschnitte erhellen die architektonische Absicht: die zeitliche Abfolge als Weg durch die Geschichte, von unten nach oben, von früher auf später (die Schulklassen mögen eingestimmt werden unten auf einer Insel im Stuttgarter Grundwasser), der grün-blau schillernde Buckel des aus dem Gartengrund aufsteigenden Glasdaches als Rücksichtnahme gegenüber dem Neuen Schloss, das nicht weiter bedrängt werden soll. Die unters Dach und in den Eingang gestellten 'Präfigurationen' beherbergen das gesamte Sonderprogramm und helfen zur Planie hin Haus zu machen, Haus der Geschichte in diesem Fall.

Haus der Geschichte, Stuttgart

1990, Axel Schultes
in Bangert Jansen Scholz Schultes
with Charlotte Frank

More a bit left over than a garden, more an area than a place – I've never fussed around so much with a volume of building that was easily manageable anyway as I did here behind the old Neues Schloss, in the approaches to Scottish-Egyptian Modernism. Schloss and Staatstheater don't make any fuss, the Landtag makes any plan awkward that tries to forge a link between the old and the very new in the garden of the Akademie. The Haus der Geschichte as a staircase over the Konrad Adenauer gorge, on the axis of the Schloss, too anxious about tidiness in the last resort? Ram a walled corner, pavilion or some rotunda-ambition into the Charlottenplatz spandrel and ultimately add to the misery? A second piano, counterpart to the Landtag, will not fit, however much you love a baroque sense of order, the Planie resists it. It would be nice – to journey from many errors to the truth – no, it's more like a modern Don'unnerstand, trying to describe traditional urban space where there isn't any.

Right then, make shallow spaces, work in layers parallel to the façade of the Schloss, they're there anyway, topographically, the Nesenbach, the old Cannstatt road, the edge of the slope. Hang on to Stirling's game with ramps for the whole edge of the slope, up to the Landesarchiv, and the double row of trees as well. The grove of plane trees shuts off the insulting sheet-metal avalanche, with two more rows of trees on the protrusion over the Bundesstrasse, if the 1987 symposium gets its own way about opposing roadside development.

The so-called garden comes on to the agenda in the next layer on the Schloss side: Landtag and Haus der Geschichte are part of the dominant belt of greenery and water between the Staatstheater and the Planie – the Land's fate and history made here and interpreted there. A promenade from Karlsplatz past the Schloss and the theatre, a counterpart to the grove of plane trees, determines the transition to the actual Schlosspark.

"In unserem Weinberg liegt ein Schatz!"
"An welchem Platz?" schrie alles gleich der Vater an.
"Grabt nur!" O weh, da starb der Mann.

("There's a treasure in our vineyard"/"Where?" they all shouted at their father at once. / "Just dig!" alas, the man then died.) History as a vineyard, a good Swabian way of bringing recalcitrant material to the public with appropriate spatial illumination. The stages and strata inside, you could interpret it like this if you felt like it, are reminiscent of the structure of the garden outside. The cross-section models illuminate the architectural intention: time sequence as a way through history, from bottom to top, from early to late (school parties can be put in the right frame of mind down below, on an island in the Stuttgart groundwater), the green-blue shimmering hump of the glass roof rises from the depths of the garden out of consideration for the Neues Schloss, which is not to be further pressured. The 'prefigurations' placed beneath the roof and in the entrance house the entire special programme and help to make a home on the Planie side, a Home for History, in this case.

zwei andere Konzepte, Antworten auf die Schlossachse   two other concepts, responses to the Schloss axis

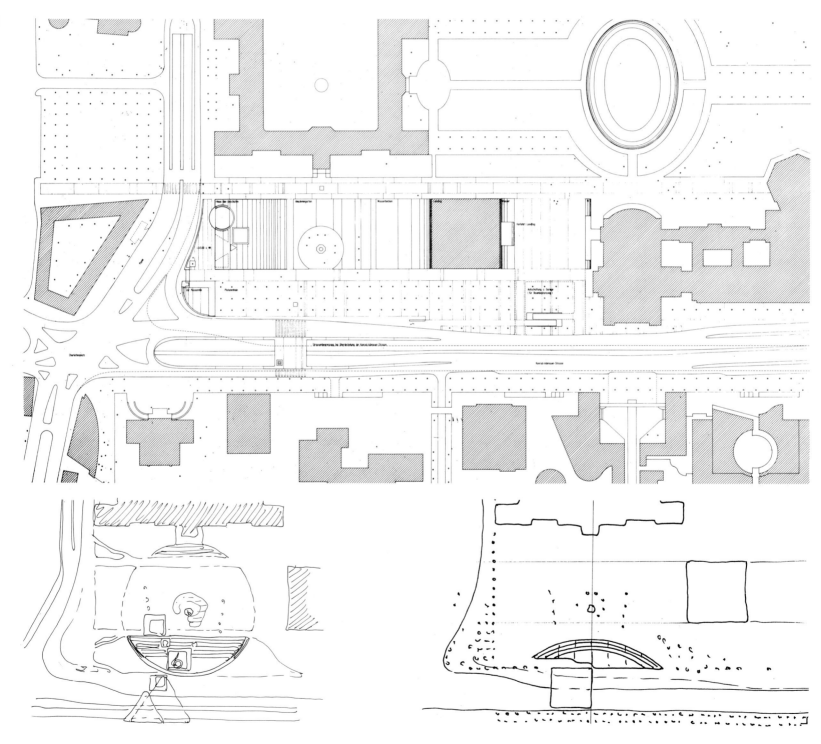

das Haus der Geschichte mit dem Neuen Schloss   Haus der Geschichte and Neues Schloss

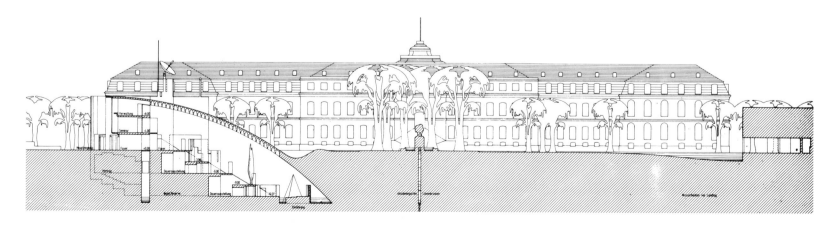

Grundriss Erdgeschoss

ground floor ground plan

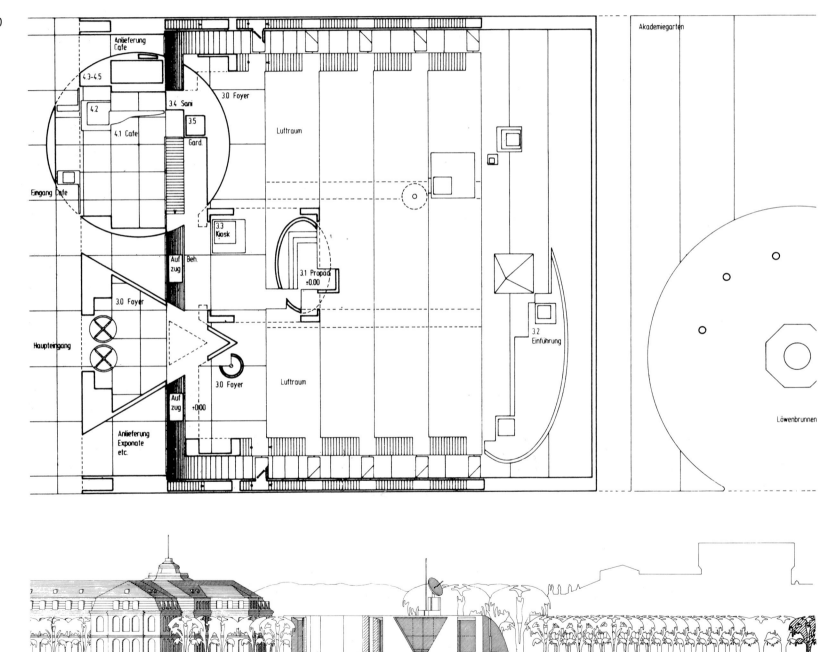

Grundriss 1. Untergeschoss

first basement ground plan

91

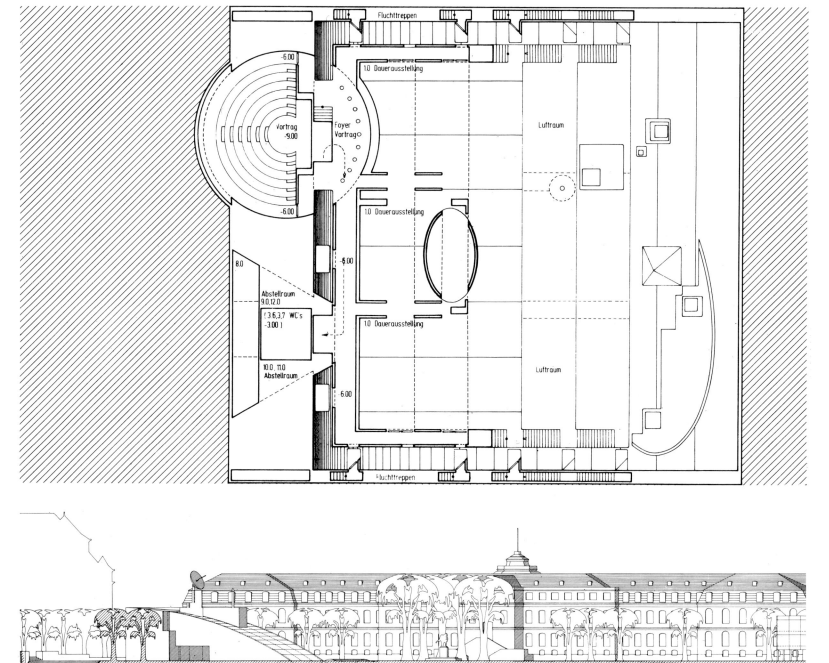

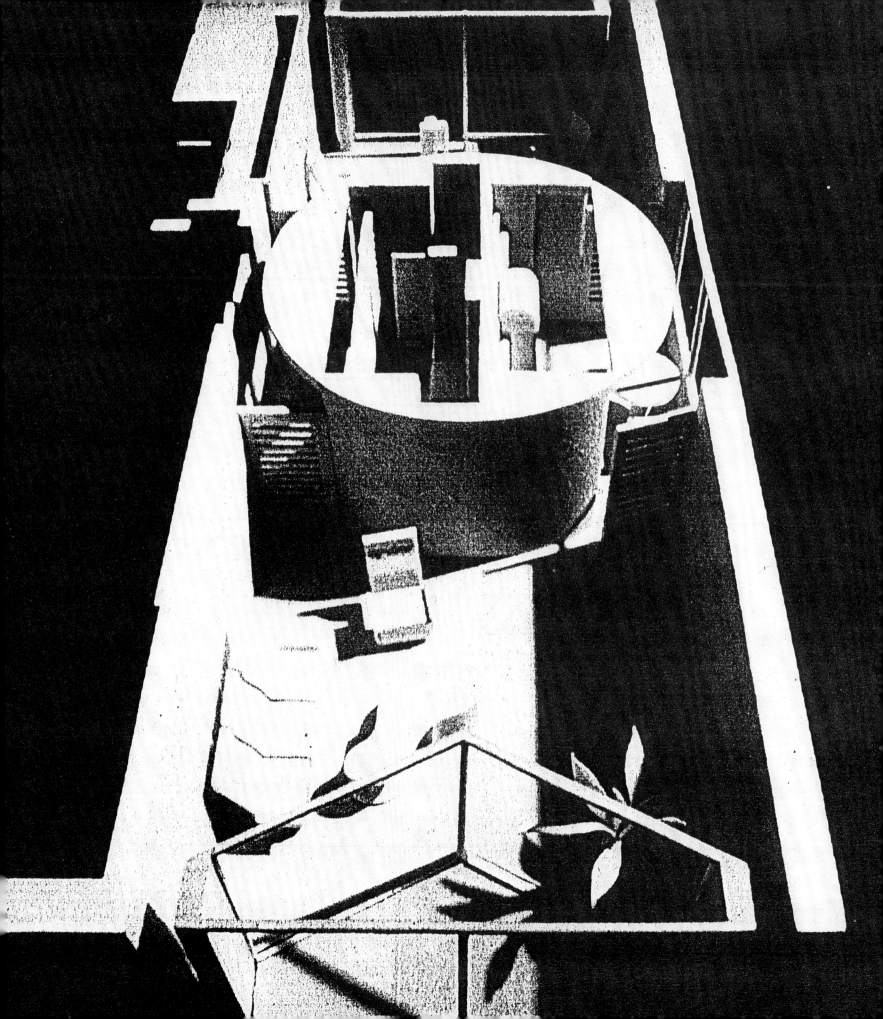

Wohnen an der Hasenheide, Berlin

1989, Axel Schultes
in Bangert Jansen Scholz Schultes
mit Charlotte Frank, Joachim Koob

Living in Hasenheide, Berlin

1989, Axel Schultes
in Bangert Jansen Scholz Schultes
with Charlotte Frank, Joachim Koob

Grosszügig sollte es schon sein, das Konzept für die Hasenheide, wenn denn Konkurrenz und Jury mehr bringen sollen als das – pardon – Gewurstel um den Werner-Düttmann-Platz. Ein geordnetes Fortschreiben der Höfe, eine Linden-Ritter-Strasse, so, wie Düsseldorf schon immer war, wird sicherlich angeboten – dem Kreuzberger Masstab treu zu bleiben, darin sehen wir die Alternative: die Zweispänner-Türme haben bis zur Maisonette Berliner Traufe, die Loggia-Höhlung darüber ist Berliner Dach. Die grüne Welle dahinter schwappt so lang wie möglich vom alten Festsaal über Restaurant und Kegeln, hinunter in die Regenwassersenke und über die Kinder drüber weg bis zur Kirche an der Privatstrasse. Die Türme im zweiten Glied lassen grosse Lücken für Kita und Wohnen dahinter (und reklamieren ein Schmalseitenprivileg für die Abstände).

Ein Hauch von Grosszügigkeit wird auch fürs Wohnen versucht: den *einen* Kern fürs Unmittelbare, für den Grundsatz, drumherum der *eine* Raum fürs übrige Leben, ein dickes Kastenfenster im Norden, eine zum Wintergarten ausbaubare Loggia im Süden (nicht schlecht auch gegen den Hasenheidener Verkehrslärm), eine Ringkopplung der Nachbarwohnung hinter Aufzug und Treppe – der Turm liesse sich bauen, wenn die Zweizimmrige die Küche über das Wohnen erschliessen darf oder, bei Kerndrehung um 90°, das Südwohnen mit Küche gekoppelt werden könnte (ich würd's mir eher so einrichten).

It certainly ought to be generous, this plan for Hasenheide, if competitors and judges are to achieve more than the, sorry, mess around Werner-Düttman-Platz. Orderly continuation of the courtyards, a Linden-Ritter-Strasse, as Düsseldorf always was, will certainly be on offer – remaining true to the scale of Kreuzberg, that's what we see as the alternative: the twin towers are the standard height for eaves in Berlin up to the maisonette, the loggia hollow above them is a Berlin roof. The green wave behind that sloshes around for as long as it can – from the old ballroom via restaurant and skittles, down into the rainwater hollow and on over the children's heads to the church in Privatstrasse. The towers in the second section leave great gaps for children's day-care centre and living behind it (and lay claim to narrow-side-on privileges for the spaces in between).

We're looking for a touch of generosity inside the apartments as well: *one* core for immediate things, for fundamentals, and around that *one* space for the rest of life, a sturdy box-type window in the north, a loggia that can be extended as a conservatory in the south (not bad to keep down the Hasenheide traffic noise either), ring link-up with the next-door flat behind lift and stairs the tower could be built if the one-bedroom flat has access to the kitchen via the living space – or by turning the core through 90°, living space facing south could be linked with the kitchen (I think that's what I'd do).

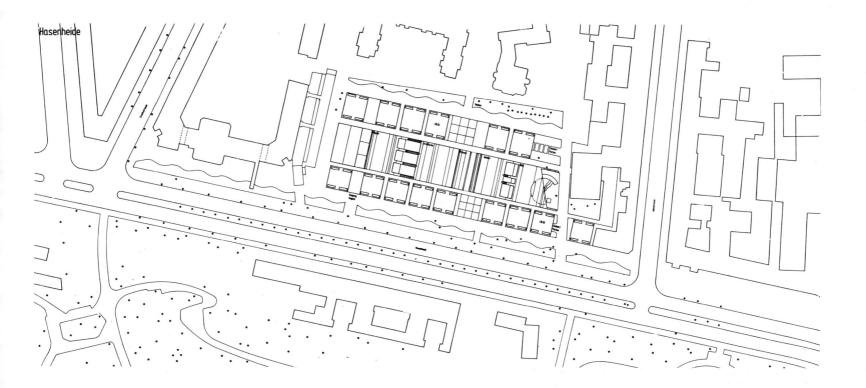

Grundriss Erdgeschoss

ground floor ground plan

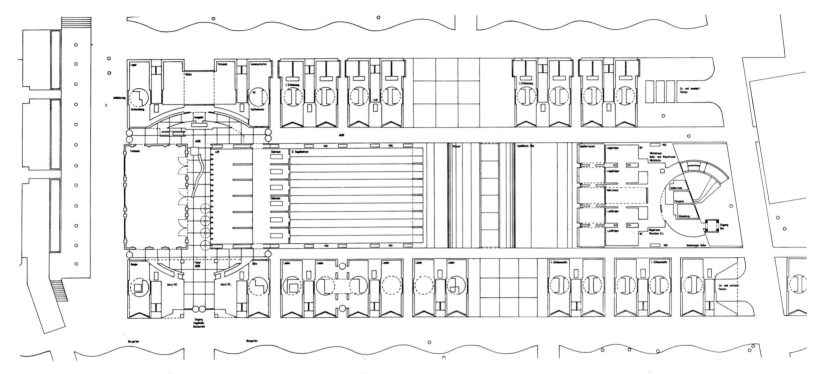

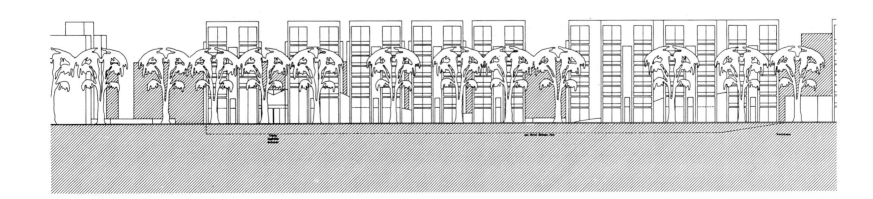

Grundriss 1. Obergeschoss   first floor ground plan

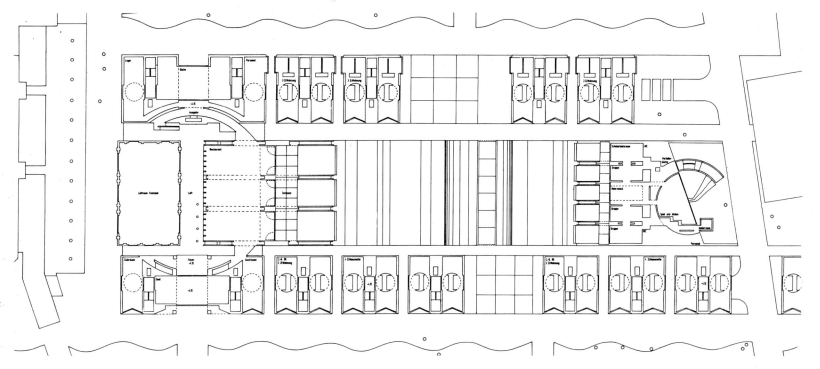

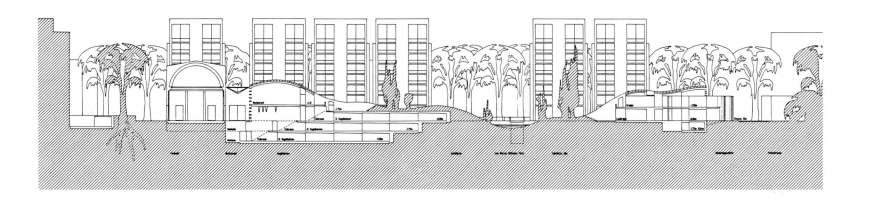

Büropark am Welfenplatz, Hannover

1989, Axel Schultes
in Bangert Jansen Scholz Schultes
mit Charlotte Frank

Im Büro sitzen ist auch Wohnen – unter anderen Umständen. Einen leergebombten Wohnblock mit 20 000 qm Bürofläche zu besetzen, heisst in Masstab und Gliederung das Visavis der Wohnbauten rücksichtsvoll umzusetzen:
– die aufgeschnittenen Quader auf dem Plateau der Tiefgarage verwandeln die kompakten 24.0 m x 24.0 m der Büroetage in – bei aller steinernen Massivität – feingliedrige Teilvolumen von 11.0 m x 11.0 m;
– die eigentlich breit lagernden Volumen mit Gebäudehöhen von 12.0 m strecken sich zu 'Wohnhaus'-Fassaden von 15.0 m Höhe bei 10.0 m Breite;
– die Pergola-Ausbildung der Attika-Zone gibt dabei die allen Bürohäusern gemeinsame Konvention, hinter der sich das stadträumlich Wünschenswerte, der individuell handhabbare Dachaufbau bis ins 7. Obergeschoss hinauf entwickeln kann.
Kein Trick – eher Methode: die steinerne Schwere der freigestellten Aussenwandelemente macht eigentliche Transparenz erst möglich – die Tiefe eines Bauvolumens jenseits aller Glaskasten-Durchsichtigkeit.

Welfenplatz office park, Hanover

1989, Axel Schultes
in Bangert Jansen Scholz Schultes
with Charlotte Frank

Sitting in an office is living as well – just under different circumstances. Fitting 20,000 sq m of office space into a bombed out residential block means taking care in transposing scale and articulation from the residential buildings opposite:
– the split ashlar on the platform of the underground garage transforms the compact 24 x 24 m of the office storey into delicate part volumes of 11 x 11 m, despite all their stone solidity;
– volumes are actually broad, with building heights of 12 m, but extend to 'residential building' façades 15 m high by 10 m wide;
– the pergola finish to the attic floor gives the convention common to all office buildings behind which what is desirable in terms of the urban space, the individually manageable building on the roof, can develop up to the seventh floor.
Not a trick – more a method: the stoney weight of the free-standing outer wall elements is actually what makes transparency possible – depth of building volume, beyond all the transparency of glass boxes.

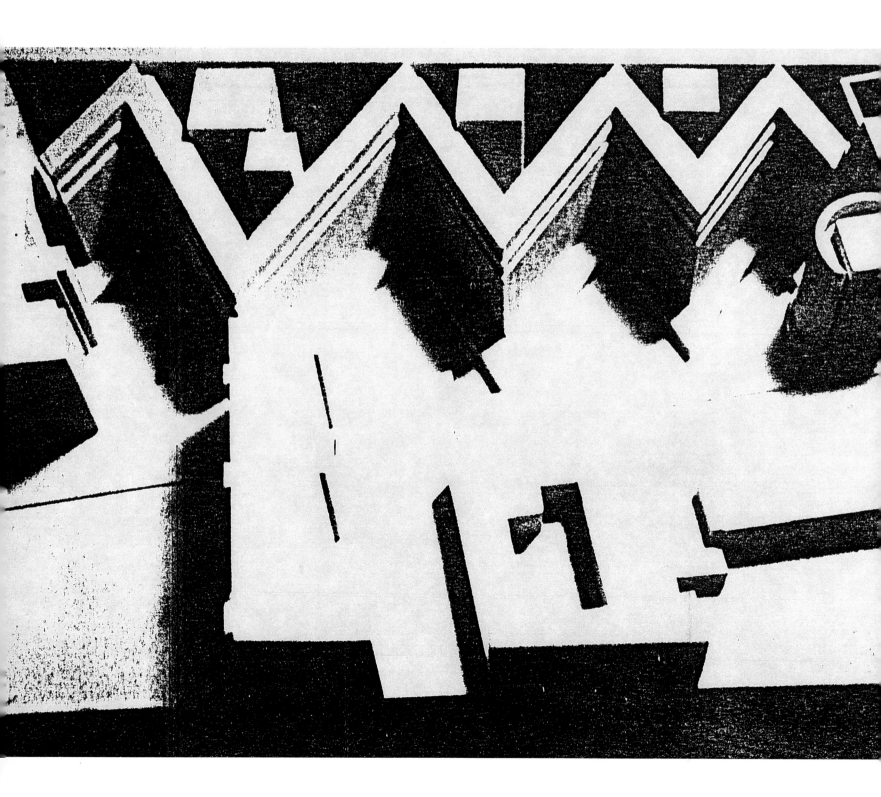

Haus am Michel, Hamburg

1989, Axel Schultes
in Bangert Jansen Scholz Schultes
with Charlotte Frank

The new Haus am Michel is to occupy the space of at least three buildings, and the Cerberus who watches over the three and three half entrances also has three heads; the zig-zag wall of the offices is also threefold and there are three and a half halls, staircases, lifts, conference-room towers and coffee corners – at least there's only one chapel. All of these are founders of the Unio Mystica of these parts of the church north of the Elbe, parts so reluctantly committed to the 'one in all'.

Transposing this 'one in all', the trinity of bishop, diaconate and mission, into a plan was the problem posed for the architects – but architectural method, town-planning requirements and not least the image of the *one* building also has programmatic consequences: if the offices, one face of the building, are orientated away from the noise, and all face the sun and the Elbe, as if they are pretending to be private like a residential area, then the public parts of the building, the halls and thus also the approaches and entrances, are committed to the town and at the mercy of the Ost-West-Strasse – the clients had to bid farewell to the image of an idyllic entrance in the town's back yard – account has to be taken of and tribute paid to the sheer, almost public size of the building and the significance of the institution – post-war Hamburg is Hamburg on the Ost-West-Strasse, not in Gerstäckerstrasse (and the quality of one's own place of work is not the last thing to benefit from this).

Grundriss Erdgeschoss

ground floor ground plan

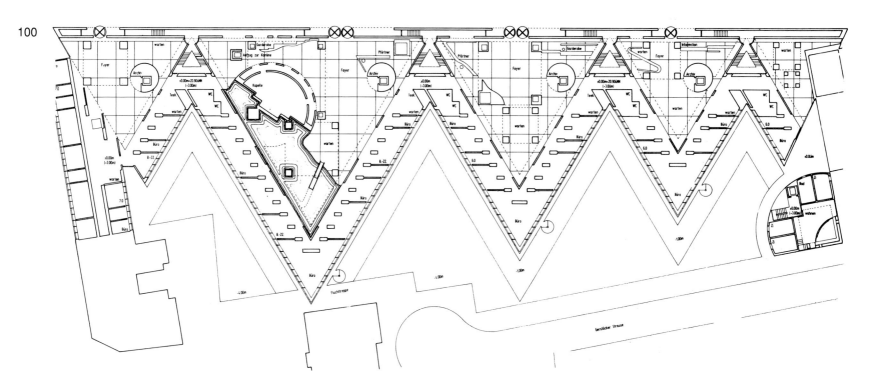

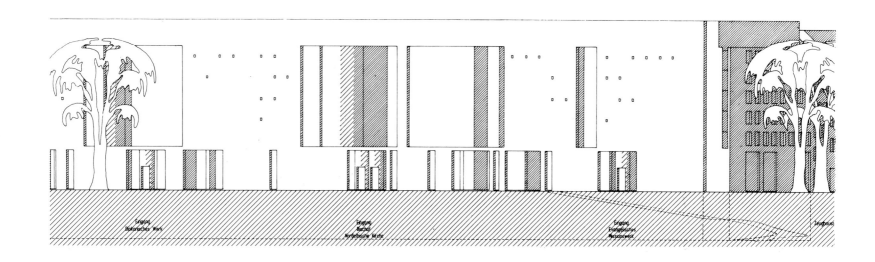

Fassade, Schnitt Büro façade, cross-section office

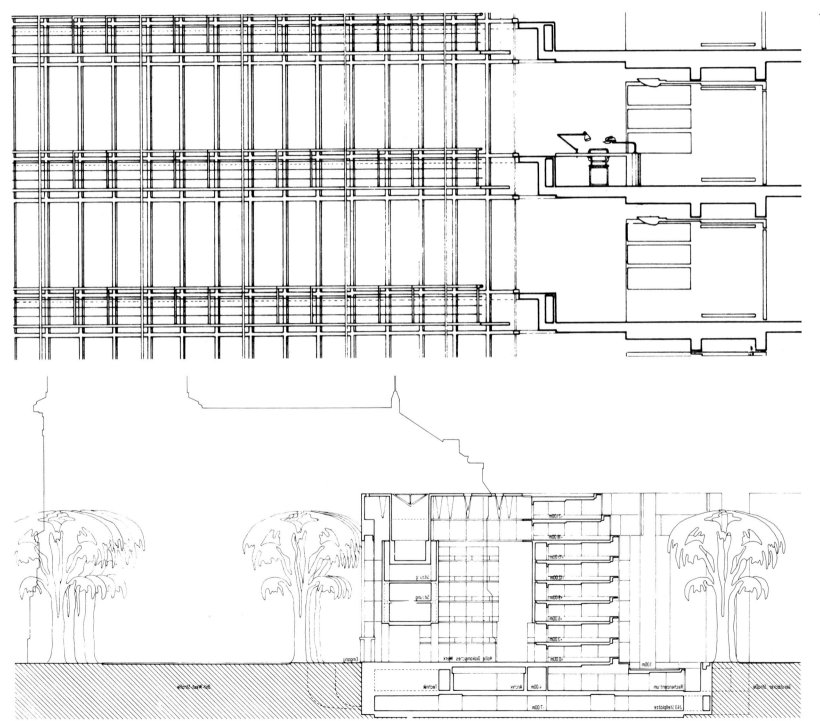

Tokyo International Forum

1989, Axel Schultes
in Bangert Jansen Scholz Schultes
with Charlotte Frank, Joachim Koob

The monotony of the Marunuchi district with its container-offices is provocative – an institution as concerned with communication and action as the Tokyo International Forum has to find another language, a language of its own; the much livelier, small-scale nature of the Ginza is no help either:

they wanted a symbol for Tokyo, but friendly, of course: it is possible to disagree about the beauty of this town, but the quiet sensitivity of old Nippon and the noisy dynamic of new Japan had to be expressed: and so one was designing here not so much against one's own conviction as against one's own prejudices: the techniques of classical cubic and spheroid architecture, as naturally applied in the halls, could not carry out this expressive function. Tokyo wants to invent itself anew on this site. Obsession with nature in the middle of a haiku is perhaps the key to this topographical architecture: here palms, papyrus and lotus are not forerunners of architectural type, the overall landscape of the place is the starting point. Depicting repose and dynamic one within the other: this intention may well lie well beyond the grasp of architecture, more like 'the art of motor-cycle maintenance'.

All the hanging gardens: foyers, restaurants, bars, cafés, seating areas; International Exchange, Metropolitan Information, exhibitions – they are all on the edges of the slope, on the open bank strips, by the river and on the hills. The stepped walls in the model are of course not walls: all the terrace edges are curtains of blue-oxided steel slats – arranged horizontally, leaving open all views and orientations over the valley and into the city, but creating contour and volume in perspective (outside the common lobby, as a façade to the plaza, these curtain walls – genuine curtain walls – are glazed).

A congress for 5,000: that's a lot of people whichever way you look at it, that is heavy traffic. The first task is to house the individual with dignity, not merely accommodate him, channel him through. Part of this is orientation of the visitor a priori, at first glance: everyone understands the workings of river and bridge, valley and hill: you have to be able to see 'up' and 'down', not just on the indicator in the lift. Everyone hates corridors – architects call them streets or even squares in big buildings – 'streets' then for 5,000 people per half hour were to be avoided, just generously designed decks and mezzanines. An open view to the outside from every room worthy of the name: something else to be taken for granted.

Two is togetherness, three is a crowd, 5,000 …, 20,000 what? For the Tokyo International Forum it can mean agoraphobia and claustrophobia in the same place and at the same time: the model photograph of the 5,000 seater hall shows how spatial intimacy and the compulsion of large numbers can go hand in hand: through spatial form developed from content; here for example the Graeco-Roman theatre adapted with reference to large-hall sight-lines and acoustics.

Massenmodell, von Osten
Grundriss Erdgeschoss

full model, from east
ground floor ground plan

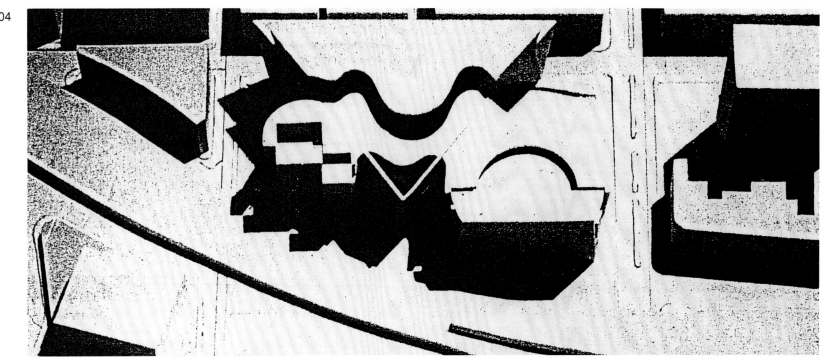

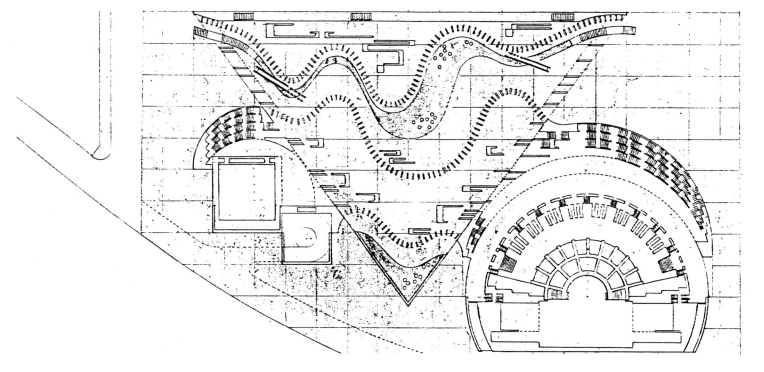

Massenmodell, Blick über Japan Rail auf die Bühnentürme full model, view across Japan Rail to fly-towers

105

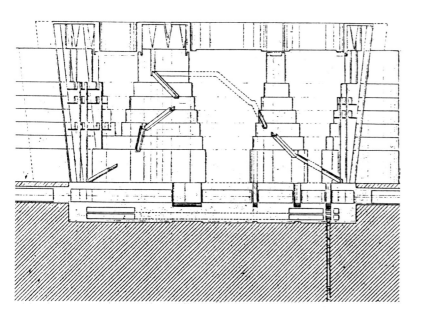

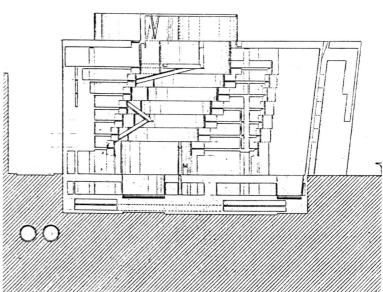

Blick in die Schlucht der Common Lobby, oberhalb Yurakucho Plaza
Detail der Common Lobby

view into Common Lobby canyon, above Yurakucho Plaza
Common Lobby detail

Blick auf die Schlucht der Common Lobby, oberhalb Keiyo Plaza
Detail der Common Lobby

view of Common Lobby canyon, above Keiyo Plaza
Common Lobby detail

die grosse Kongresshalle, 5000 Sitzplätze

the large 5,000-seater congress hall

Konzeptkomponenten: Lobby mit Rolltreppen, Hangkante mit Dach

concept components: Lobby with escalators, slope edge with roof

Internationaler Seegerichtshof, Hamburg

1989, Axel Schultes
in Bangert Jansen Scholz Schultes
mit Charlotte Frank, Joachim Koob

Wie kommt die UNO nach Nienstedten, wie kommt die Villa Schröder an die UNO? Wie das Lokale, das Haus und Grundstück Bürgerstolz, mit den 150 'Signatarstaaten' unserer Weltrettungsgesellschaft ins Benehmen setzen? Die herrlichen alten Bäume werden's schon richten – so hoffen wir alle.

Aber im Ernst: die erste UNO-Dependance in der Bundesrepublik ist eigener und fremder als die Georg-Bonne-Strasse sich träumen lässt – bei allem Harmoniebedürfnis der Stadtoberen: der Seegerichtshof macht sich's nicht bequem hinter einer Villa, die man schon mit sehr viel Liebe anschauen muss – er macht sich seinen eigenen Ort, sucht sich sein eigenes Territorium: 90 m x 90 m inklusive Villa Schröder – der Elbhang, die alten Bäume, die lieben Nachbarn, alles das bleibt aussen vor: die UNO steckt den Claim ab, in aller Freundschaft, versteht sich.

Auf diesem knappen Hektar sammelt sich die Rechtsfindung:
– die Villa, um zwei Präsidentensuiten erweitert, schaut dann hoffentlich, wenn schon nicht herrschaftlich, so doch etwas öffentlicher drein (der Denkmalpfleger wird's zu würdigen wissen!);
– der Gerichts-'Hof' gibt die Statur – und pomp and circumstances dazu – für die Herren Diplomaten in ihren schwarzen Limousinen (Entwerfen ist wohl immer: so tun, als wenn's wahr wäre);
– die grosse Halle (Grosszügigkeit fordert die Ausschreibung – welcher Kollege lässt sich das zweimal sagen), die grosse Halle also gibt sich viel Mühe mit ihrer Diagonalen: im Dreieck zur Villa präsentiert sie das Öffentliche mit Sälen und der ganzen Logistik, im Winkel gegenüber die tagtägliche Plackerei im Büro; die lange Treppe hilft bei der Rechtssuche;
– die Kopplung repräsentativer Räume läuft immer auf einen Kompromiss hinaus: Ausgangspunkt des Saalkonzeptes hier beim Auditorium war eine Subtraktion – der grösste Raum, das wichtigste Ereignis soll die konsistenteste Räumlichkeit erhalten; die davon abtrennbaren Räume, hier die beiden kleinen Sitzungssäle müssen sich fügen – keine Quadrätel-Addition, das Teilbar-Eine ist Ausgangspunkt. Zwei riegelförmige, solide Hubwände mit allem Aufwand, der dazugehört, keine Falt-Klapp-Schiebe-Provisorien, machen's möglich. Zwischen den Zylinderschalen soll die AV-Technik – dolmetschen, TV etc. – untergebracht werden.

Alles das natürlich vom Standort der Villa entwickelt, wenn sie denn schon bleiben soll: ein frischeres Stück Architektur liesse sich dann irgendwann einmal finden.

Die Erweiterung legt sich da auf die Wiese, wo die Bäume noch ein bisschen Platz gelassen haben – solange die alte Platane steht, ist an einen Büroriegel hinter der westlichen Hofwand nicht zu denken?

International Tribunal for the Law of the Sea, Hamburg

1989, Axel Schultes
in Bangert Jansen Scholz Schultes
with Charlotte Frank, Joachim Koob

How can we bring the UN to Nienstedten, how can Villa Schröder relate to the UN? How can we put something so local, a would-be petit bourgeois residence, in touch with our Save the World Company? The splendid old trees will do the trick: that's what we all hope.

Seriously though: the first UN branch in the Federal Republic is stranger and more alien than Georg-Bonne-Strasse's wildest dreams – however much the city fathers call for harmony: the Maritime Court isn't going to be comfortable behind a villa we really have to look at with a great deal of affection – the court will make its own place, seeks its own territory: 90 x 90 m including Villa Schröder – the slope to the Elbe, the old trees, the dear neighbours, all that stays outside: the UN is staking its claim, a friendly claim, of course.

Justice collects itself on this bare hectare:
– the villa, extended by two presidential suites, we hope will then look, if not splendid, a little more public (the keeper of monuments will certainly appreciate it?!)
– the court itself provides the correct status – and pomp and circumstance as well – for diplomats in their black limousines (designing always means: act as if it were true)
– the great hall (the brief demands scale – which of our colleagues would need telling twice) the great hall therefore takes a lot of trouble with its diagonal: in a triangle to the villa it presents the public face with courtrooms and all the logistics, in the opposite angle the everyday office grind; the long staircase aids the search for justice.
– linking representative spaces always ends in compromise: the starting point for the room concept of the auditorium here was a subtraction – the largest room, the most important event, is intended to have the most coherent space; rooms that can be separated from it, here the two small courts, have to fit in – no little square additions, divisible oneness is the starting point. This is achieved by using two solid, barrier walls that can be raised, with all the expense associated with this, no provisional stuff that folds or pushes aside. Audio-visual technology – interpreters' equipment, TV etc. – is accommodated between the cylinder shells.

All this developed from the villa, if it really is here to stay: a fresher bit of architecture could be found some time or another.

The extension is placed on the grass where the trees have left a bit of room – as long as the old plane tree stands we probably can't consider a run of offices beyond the western wall of the court?

Blick über das Foyer auf die grosse Serpentine
Blick über das Elbufer nach Norden

view across foyer to great bend
view over the bank of the Elbe to the north

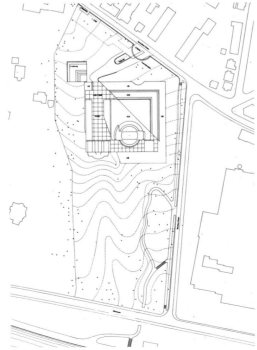

Blick über das Foyer auf den Sitzungssaal	view across foyer to courtroom
Grundriss Erdgeschoss	ground floor ground plan
Grundriss 2. Obergeschoss	2nd floor ground plan
Grundriss 4. Obergeschoss	4th floor ground plan

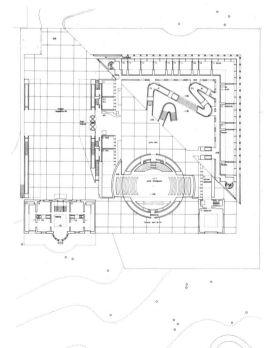
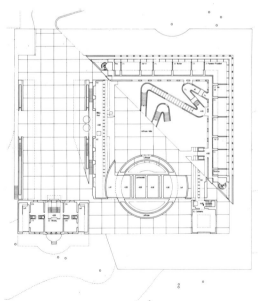
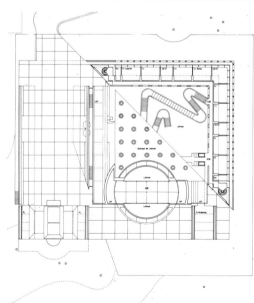

Modellschnitt durch Foyer und Gerichts-Hof

model section through foyer and court

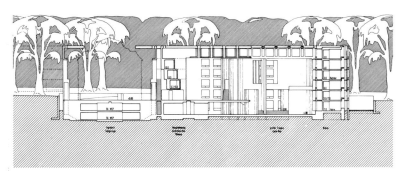
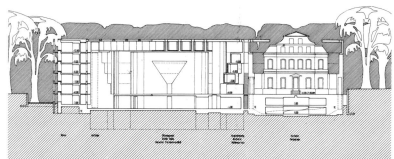

Blick vom Elbufer auf die Süd-Fassaden

view of south facades from bank of Elbe

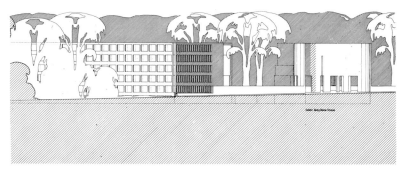

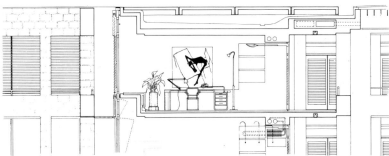

Bibliotheca Alexandrina

1989, Axel Schultes
in Bangert Jansen Scholz Schultes
with Charlotte Frank

'oh Mother Nut, spread your wings over me
like the everlasting stars'
Tut Anch Amun, on his tomb in Thebes
'the Greeks are children'
ancient Egyptian view of life.

It is worth planting an apple tree an hour before the end of the world; it is worth attempting to provide architecture for a library which if it had been saved could bear witness against our ruined Christian and post-Christian civilization. The basis of these books, a longing for eternity, is a dream that has always been part of architecture as well – the longing for infinity in this medium that is so finite, so lithophile, or in the words of Louis Kahn: silence and light as the origins of architecture.

Silence and light – that would be the law under which the new, old library could take its bow: the architect's task to pour the experience of ancient Egypt, the source of all our experience of architecture, into new, spatial parables.

The site is an inspiration in itself: overlooking antique waters, looking across to successor civilizations in the north, who even at the time of the ancient Alexandrina translated Egyptian perceptions into exploitable, western-aggressive science, means planning to do both: opening and closing, cutting and putting together, a seam in every sense, that would be an architectural gestalt for the Alexandrina.

In structural terms it would look like this: 'Ptolemy space', both square and building, is an island in a new Sea of Lotus Flowers, and places the institution – the great arch overlooking the sea for general things (conferences, services, museums, theatre, exhibition), the triangular square of the Alexandrina and the lotus ground plan of the Mubarak Center for special occasions: the water points the way to the Mediterranean for both institutions, the museum arch withholds the excessively lavish gesture, takes its own under protection.

Collected knowledge, the Alexandrina books, dispersed for long enough and now assembled around *one* room, occupying the tiers of *their* theatre – books and readers are both actors and audience. Callimachus Hall is a scene within this picture, at the back the stepped wall of the Rare Book Collection, the two Callimachus towers for the most precious of these books and documents. The five cataracts of the Great Staircase lead to the many, the far too many, the 3.5 million volumes and periodicals in the standard library; the stacks are at the back of the relevant reading areas.

In sunbles Egypt it's a pleasure to allow light to filter through into this silent world of books: flat as the body of Mother Nut in ancient temples are all the roofs of the Alexandrina, dark blue, sown with golden stars, lamp spindles collect the sunlight, channel and filter it through the stone ceilings, distribute it as they received it.

'The visitor should be struck by the silence of the place' said the brief – the model photographs show just that, and the images should be read correctly: the helpless reason of the Renaissance and its remakes, down to provisionally final Post-Modernism about five years ago, must have a stop – modern building of this century, often tried and tested only structurally or three-dimensionally, must at last find a way to suggestive spatiality: the only quality made available to architects by our industrial age that can create something new, something different, to stand alongside 'ancient building in stone', the wonders of Saqqara and Giza.

Massenmodell, der Hafen mit der Corniche im Norden, unten
Blick auf die Leseterrassen mit der grossen Treppe

full model, harbour with Corniche to the north, below
view of reading terraces and great staircase

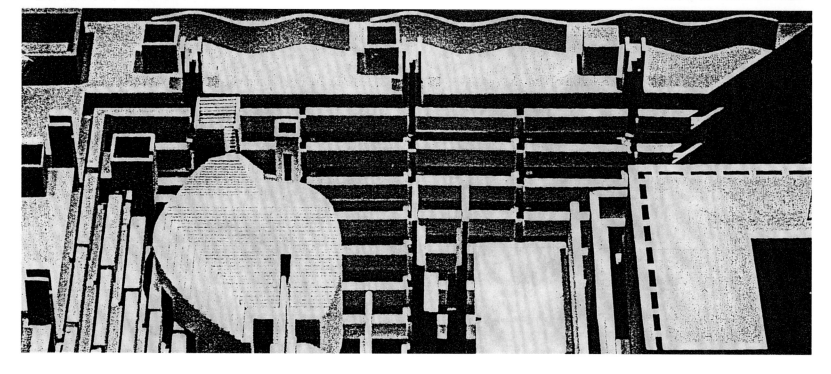

Grundriss Erdgeschoss ground floor ground plan

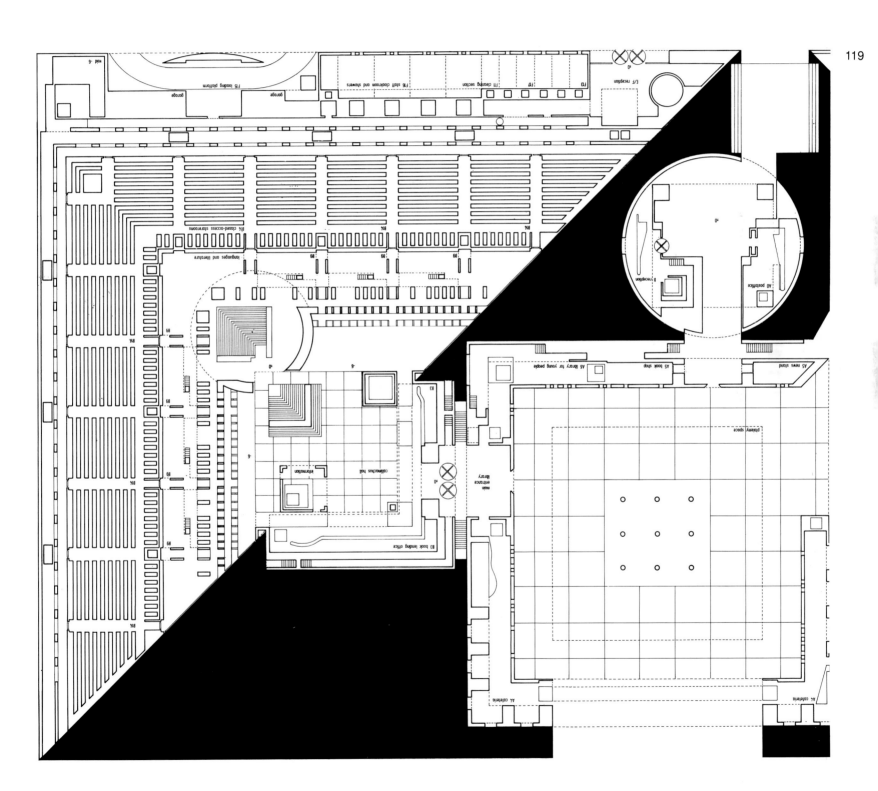

Modellschnitt von der Alexandrina bis zum Mubarak-Kongresszentrum
Detail der Decke mit Tageslichtspindeln

model cross-section of the Alexandrina to the Mubarak CongressCentre
detail of ceiling with daylight spindles

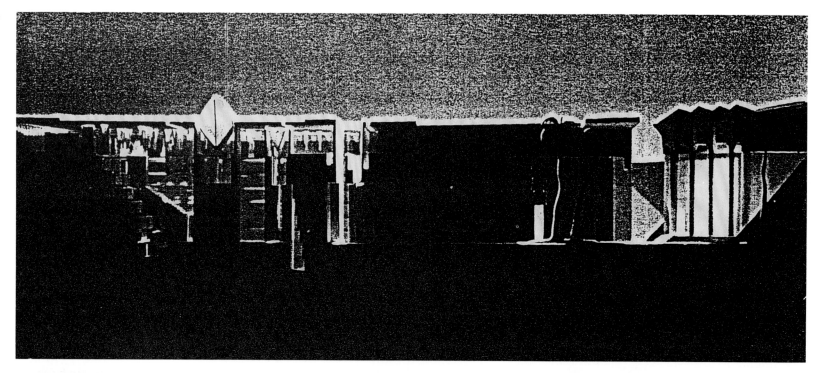

Modellschnitt, Türme und Kragfassade der Rare-Book-Collection im Vordergrund
Detail des Turm-Oberlichts

model cross-section, towers and cantilever facade of the Rare Book Collection in the foreground
detail of tower skylight

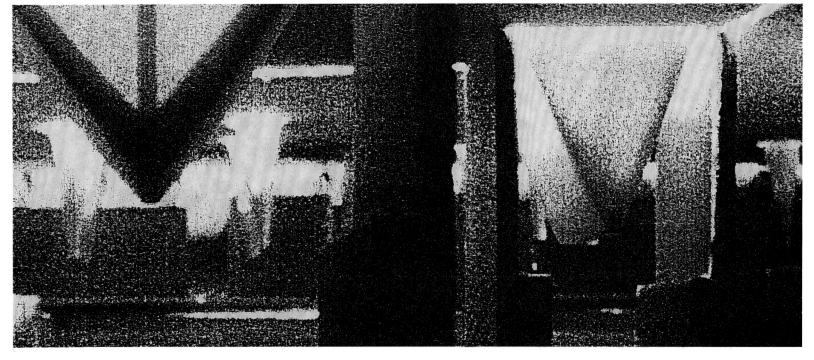

Modellschnitt, Haupteingang der Alexandrina model cross-section, Alexandrian main entrance

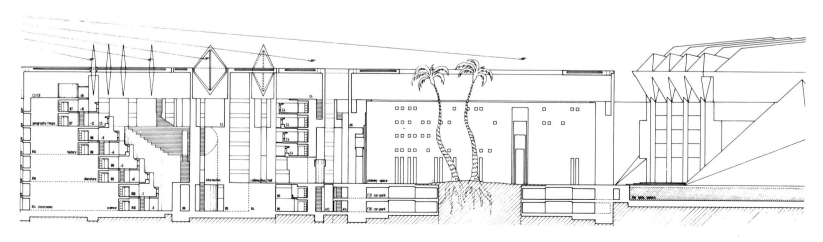

Modellschnitt, das afrikanische Zimmer – Ptolemy Space   model cross-section, African Room – Ptolemy Space

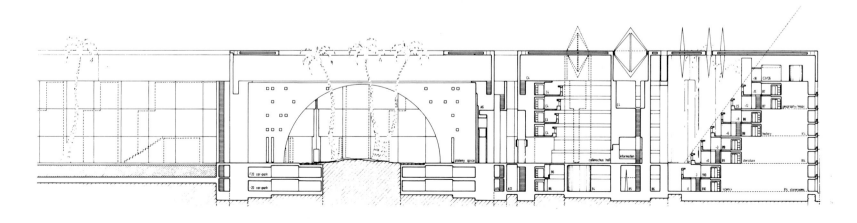

Berlin Museum

1989, Axel Schultes
in Bangert Jansen Scholz Schultes
with Charlotte Frank

If it's worth doing it's worth doing well – the building is a difficult one to play anyway, all the limits imposed by the fact that it's listed make it difficult to extend and be played, continuing the schizophrenic quality of the entrances, ways around the museum, and chronology of the exhibition levels means helplessly making things even worse, doubling something provisional – it certainly does not need the 'unusual solution' expected in the brief: all one can do is to give each his own, the Kollegienhaus to the colleagues, in other words to the directors and organizers of the building, and the museum building to the museum, i. e. foyer, exhibition and store.

The advantages are obvious:
– no bridge, nothing: the new building proposal avoids predictable squabbling between administrators of culture and the building, between curators of monuments and museum directors; the lapidarium under Hollmannstrasse can easily handle the 'small quantity of museum business';
– the rooms in the old building contain conventional things, as they did 250 years ago: everyday office work including writing, correspondence, reading and conferring. The heavy wooden portal would cover that, access to directorate and library, to the graphics collection. Even a building like this could be opened for museum visitors – but only with a crowbar – that's not what it's meant for.
– the new building on the other hand is thoroughbred exhibition architecture. Café and museum shop and auditorium wide open to Lindenstrasse and Alte-Jakob-Strasse: hardly a façade, more an interior in contrast with the worthy stone next to it.

Does the plan have a snag? Is a Biedermeier room in a pseudo-baroque environment more at home than the nineteenth-century worker's living kitchen amidst the 21st century in the new building? It seems to me simpler and more attractive to work out the characteristic features of these periods for the time-travelling visitor within the repose of a coherent spatial concept, and techncial facilities for exhibitions would then be generally available. I thus fear only one thing: the inertia of an established exhibition in established rooms: 'old to old and new to new', as it was put in the colloquium, is only marginally plausible.

The interior façades look heavy and stony in the cross-section model, but they are variable-transparent slat constructions which help to adapt light and view, or reshape the exhibition area – thus no Egyptian corridor between the two exhibition tracts is intended, there should be *one* space between the outer walls, from the bottom to the top storey; the top floor with the staircase walls is the second, very solid cover.

The museum concept was, of course, dictated by urban design necessities – there is, alas, no city south of the Berlin Museum, or it has not yet become a city again. Thus the museum quietens only the provisional southern limit of the Victoria block, but could extend to Alte-Jakob-Strasse in the long term.

126

Modellschnitt in der Längsachse   model cross-section in longitudinal axis

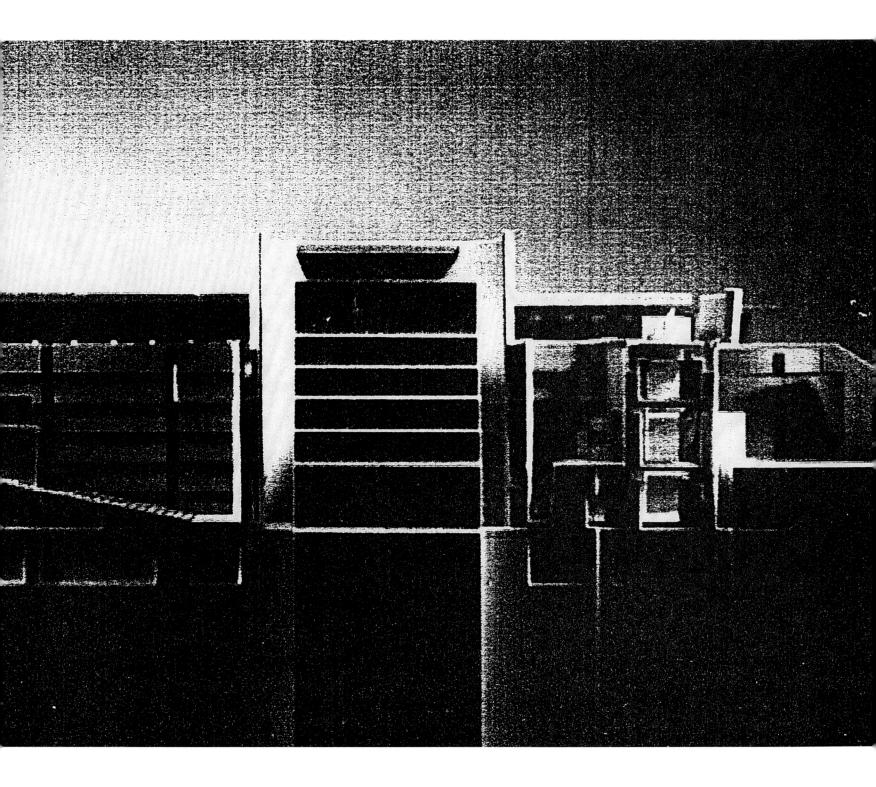

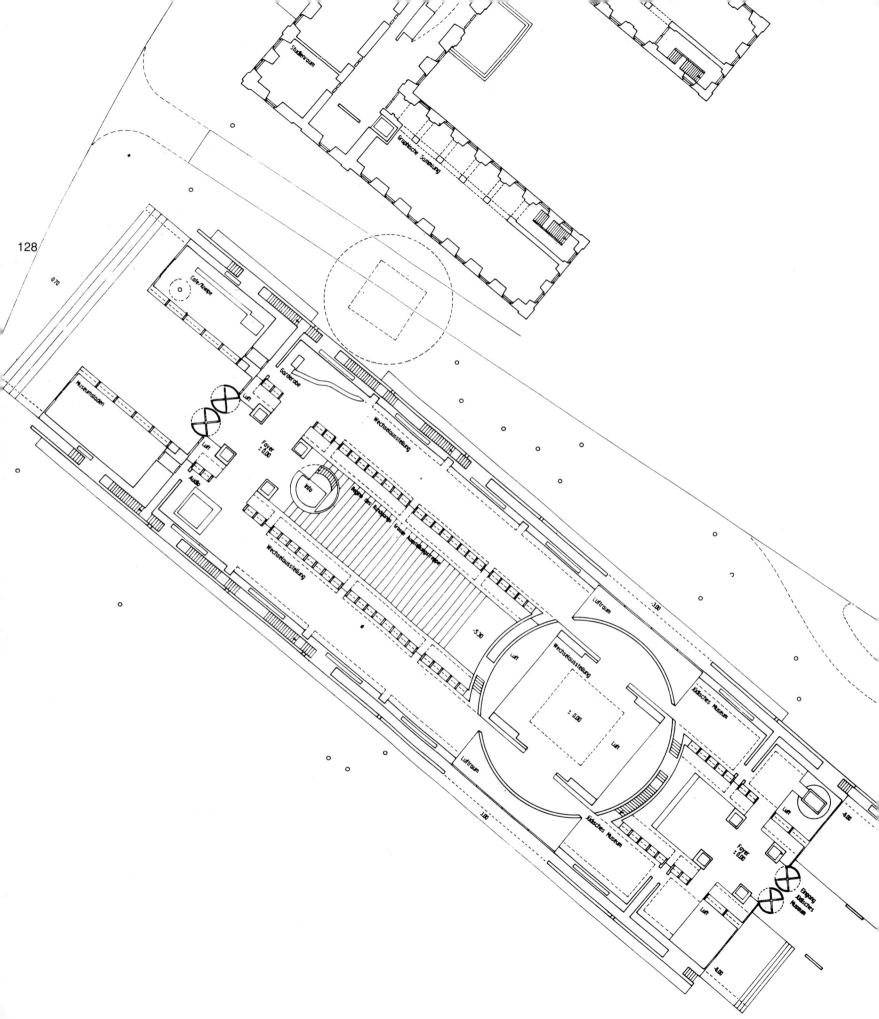

Grundriss Erdgeschoss
Modellschnitt Café, Museumsladen und Vortragssaal

ground floor ground plan
model cross-section café, museum shop and lecture hall

Blick vom Garten am Berlin Museum
Grundriss Sockelgeschoss

view of Berlin Museum from garden
base storey ground plan

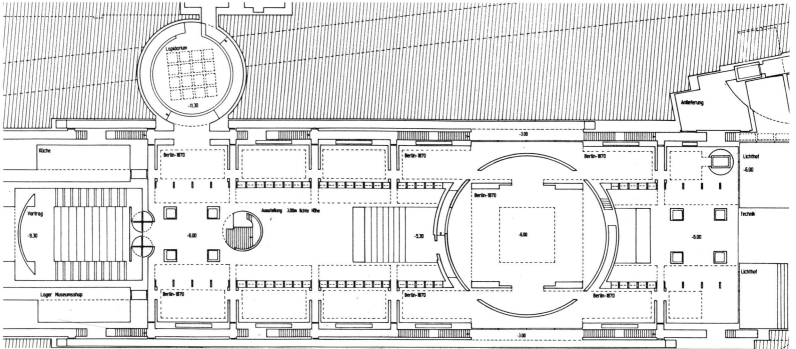

Blick von der Lindenstrasse
Grundriss 1. Obergeschoss

view from Lindenstrasse
1st floor ground plan

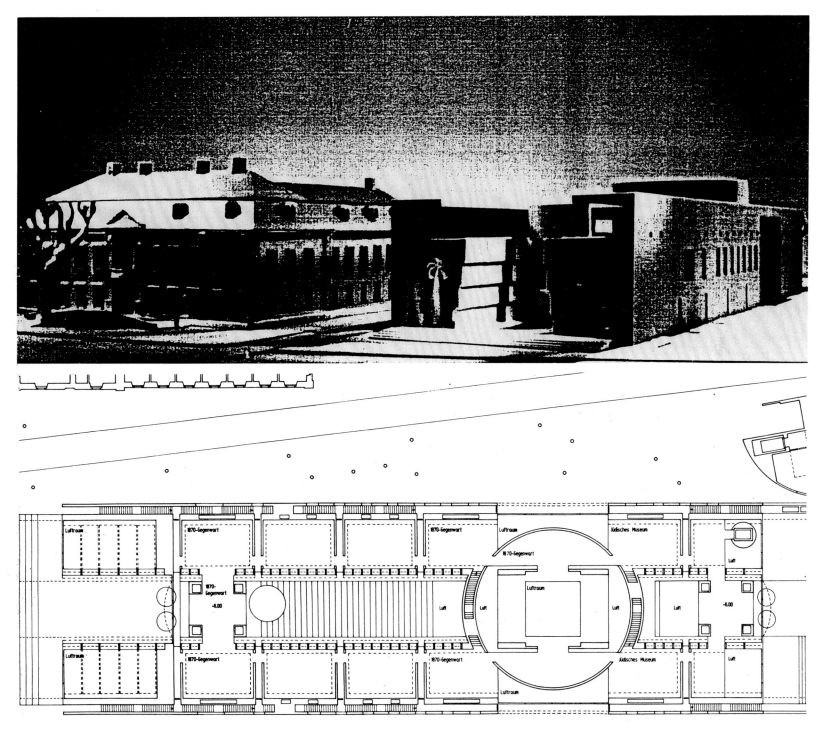

New roof at 7 Lützowplatz, Berlin

1989, Axel Schultes
in Bangert Jansen Scholz Schultes
with Charlotte Frank

A square that isn't a square want to become one: the IBA buildings on the east side of Lützowplatz are taking shape, and '7 LP' wants to join in: the post-war roof is removed, and replaced with three studio flats as a freely differentiated roofscape above an even more simplified, taut old façade.

And so the side of the square up to Einemstrasse will almost blithely reflect the modernest of the Modern: a good solid corner from Botta, a colourful breach by Cook/Baller, austere, sunken-eyed maisonettes from Schultes, a slightly noisy little skyline for 7 LP, the Haus am Lützowplatz the only 19th century offering, Hilmer/Sattler's new building a bit of the 50s – but overall certainly more town than the monotonous kitchen window group oposite. Thus the new roofs on the Galerie Poll are more of a 'why not' than an 'either-or' in our incredibly beautiful city.

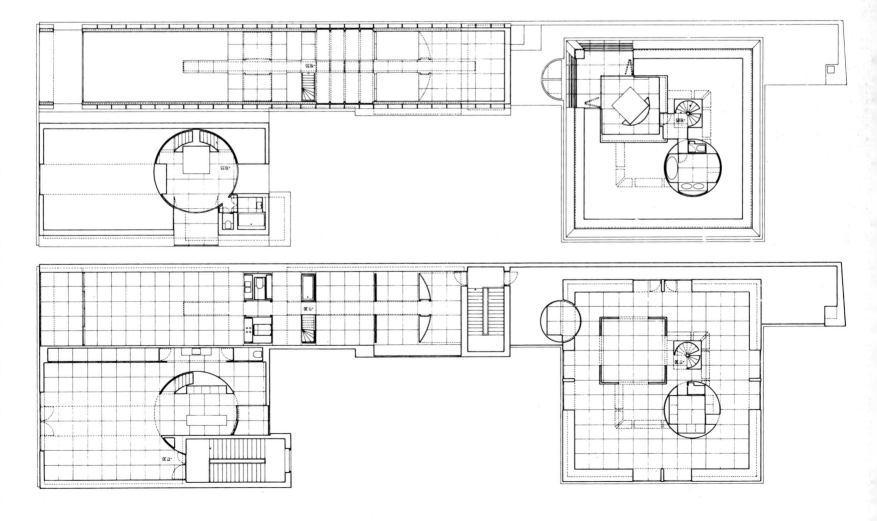

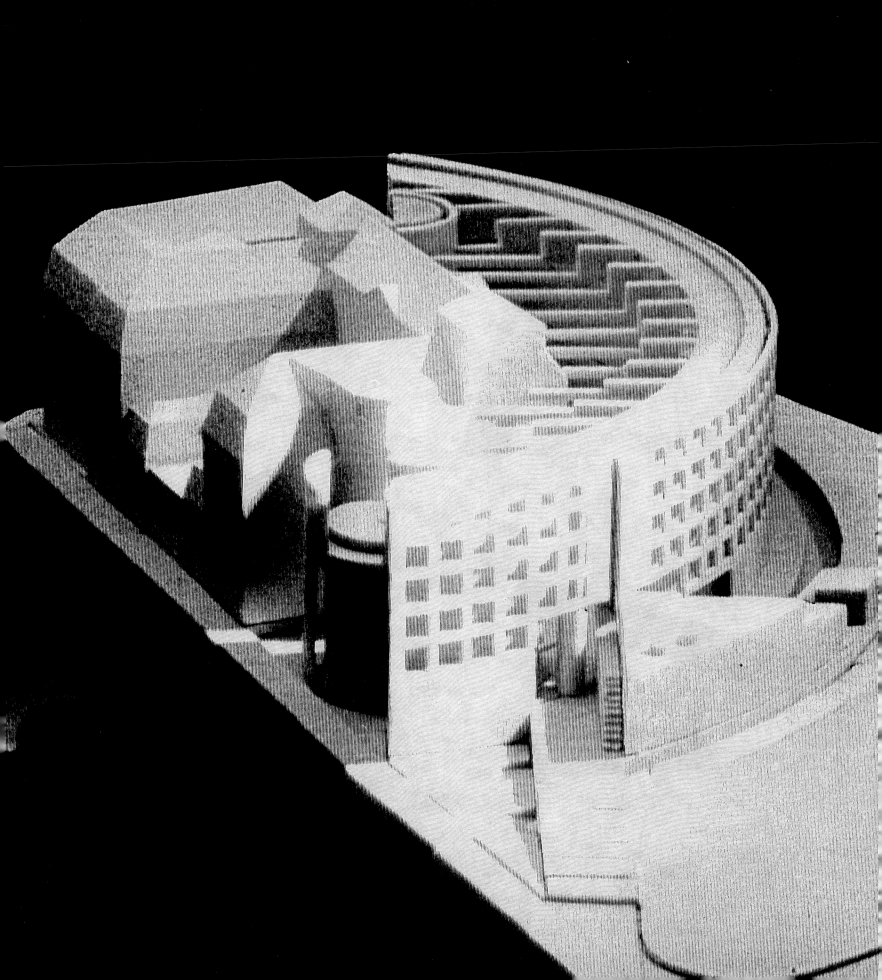

Family Court, Berlin

1989, Axel Schultes
in Bangert Jansen Scholz Schultes
with Charlotte Frank

Putting the new building, kindly as it were, next to the old courthouse as the last remainder of a block destroyed in the war, or completing a block that isn't a block in the best IBA style: that would be 'no teeth in your mouth but whistling in church'.

The new family court building has to achieve something else and more: it must complement the old building in such a way
– that the remainder of the block is enhanced to become a solitaire, effective in the urban landscape, rounded off to a new, compressed block;
– that both, the old and the new building, make *one* place, draw up *one* law around the hall in the old and in the new building;
– that the new building reformulates the loveless and threatening courtyard façades, dragged into light when the block was destroyed, and now again overlooking the common hall, and makes them gallery-like interior façades;
– that it is possible for the green areas to grow together as a park-like area as a result of concentrated, minimal extra building.

The somewhat luxurious-seeming single-loaded quality of the new building, naturally a fundamental condition of the concept and mirror image of the old building, is intended to do one thing above all, together with the hall as high as the building: an 'a priori orientation' throughout the court building, transparency of spatial organization for parties to cases, always unfamiliar with the area – I'm sure I don't need to say that this is the key to the plan: to make a place that uses architectural means to take away the burden, a place that precisely does not increase the pressure that anyway bears down upon 'seekers after justice'.

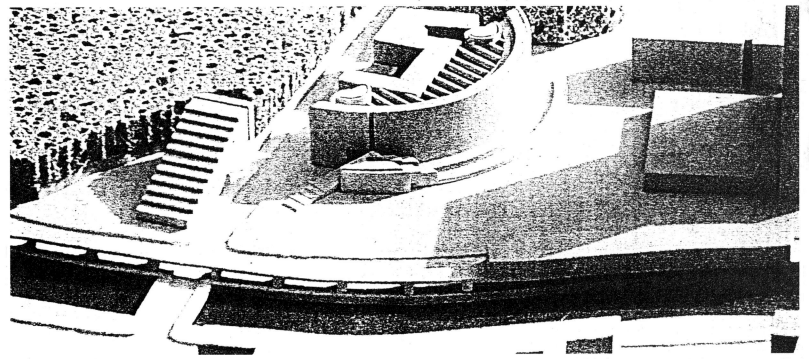

Grundriss Sockelgeschoss
Grundriss Erdgeschoss

base storey ground plan
ground floor ground plan

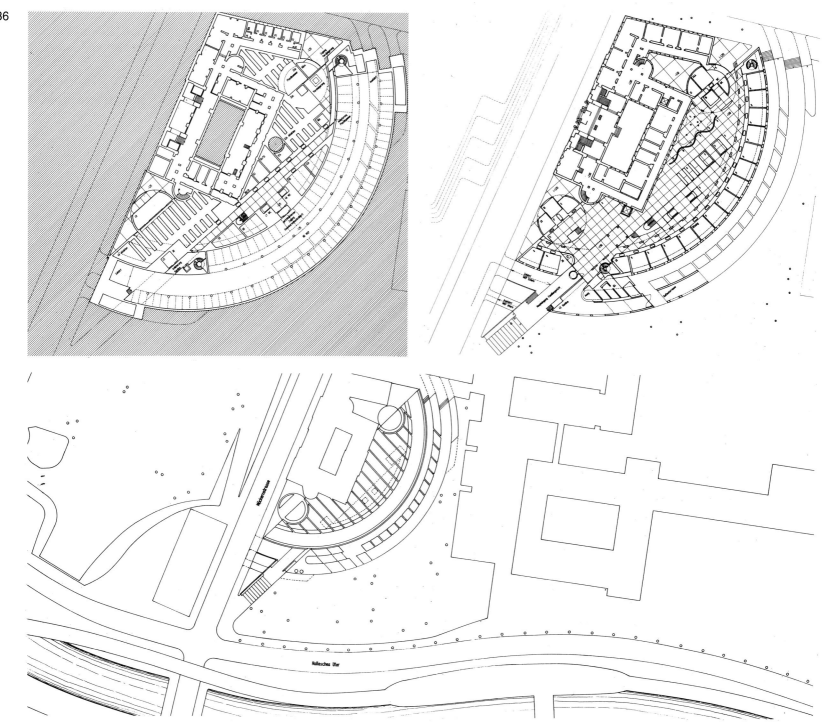

Grundriss 1. Obergeschoss
Grundriss 2. Obergeschoss

1st floor ground plan
2nd floor ground plan

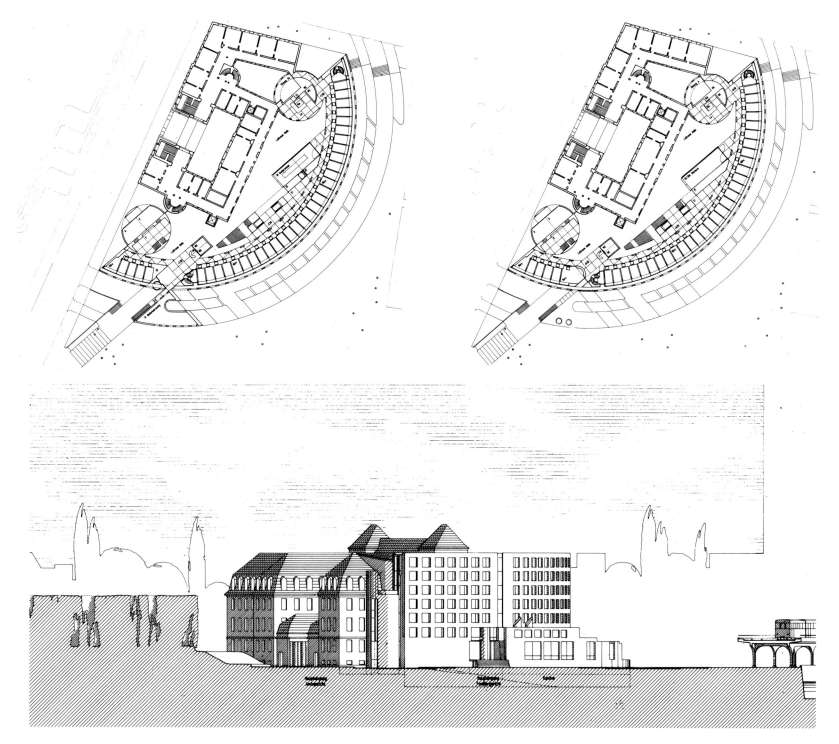

Intercity-Hotel, Berlin

1988, Axel Schultes, Stefan Scholz
in Bangert Jansen Scholz Schultes
mit Charlotte Frank

Collage-City ist überall in Berlin: absurdes Architektur-Theater, da wo noch nicht einmal Stadt ist, zum Beispiel neben der Nationalgalerie und jetzt auch am Spreebogen – oder eher tragikomisch, unfreiwillig, wie hier hinter dem Bahnhof Zoo, 20 Jahre vor Colin Rowes Bestseller.

Hier kann mit dem Neubau des Hotels Collage sinnreich eingesetzt werden: Ort und Ordnung gewonnen werden aus dem Nachkriegschaos dieser Gegend. Hier mag Türme bauen und die Beziehungslosigkeit des Vorhandenen ins Schmerzhafte steigern wer will – nicht den Konflikt unbekümmert vorführen, lieber das Alte mit ins Neue hinüberretten, der Vorschlag hier könnte es leisten:

– nicht höher als Verwaltungsgericht und Theater – ein Bundesbahnhotel sollte seinen Hang zum Horizontalischen, zu Schiene und Strecke, und zum Dynamischen, zu Rapidité und Fernweh nicht verleugnen;

– das Hotel übernimmt die Kurvatur des Gleiskörpers und der Bahnhöfe: Intercity, 'zwischen den Städten', ist auch seine Baukörpersprache und -position, dritter Bahnhof am Zoo, nach den Zügen aus dem Westen Ausschau haltend, selbst ein bisschen Zug;

– und natürlich keine zweite Fassade neben dem Theater des Westens, keine Stadtreparatur, solitär darf's schon sein im Sinne des Teils zum Ganzen.

Intercity-Hotel, Berlin

1988, Axel Schultes, Stefan Scholz
in Bangert Jansen Scholz Schultes
with Charlotte Frank

Collage City is everywhere in Berlin: absurd architecture-playacting where there isn't even any city, beside the National Gallery for example, and now on the bend of the Spree as well – perhaps it's more of a tragicomedy, involuntary, as here behind Bahnhof Zoo, 20 years before Colin Rowe's bestseller.

Here the new hotel building can permit meaningful collage: a sense of place and order emerge from the post-war chaos of this area. Here anyone who wishes may build towers, increasing the unconnectedness of what is already here to the point of pain – don't carry on the conflict as if you don't care, it's better to rescue the old and take it with you into the new, this suggestion could bring that off:

– no higher than the Court of Adminstration and the theatre – a railway hotel should not deny its inclination to the horizontal, to rails and journeys, to the dynamic, to singing speed and a longing for faraway places;

– the hotel takes on the curve of rails and stations: Intercity, 'between the cities' is also the language the building speaks and the position it occupies, third Zoo station, looking out for trains from the west, a bit of a train itself;

– and of course no second façade next to the Theater des Westens, no urban repair, let's have a building on its own, a part of the whole.

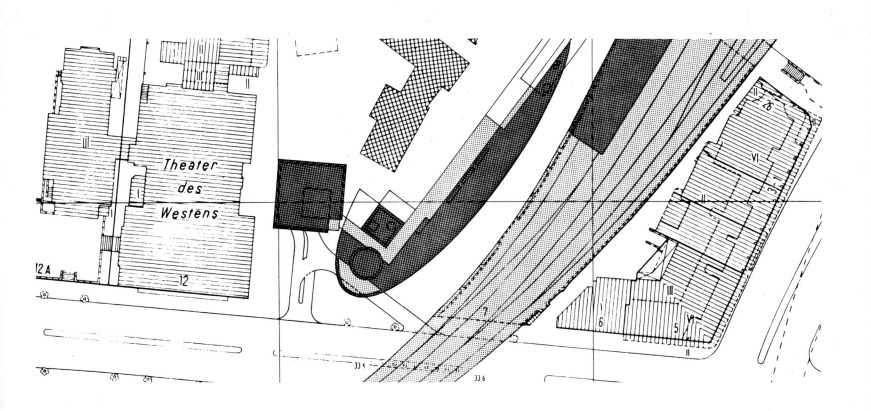

Parlamentsvorzone Bonn

1988, Axel Schultes
in Bangert Jansen Scholz Schultes

Zone outside the parliament building in Bonn

1988, Axel Schultes
in Bangert Jansen Scholz Schultes

'Zone' ist der vom Auslober genannte Arbeitstitel für die Suche nach einem Ort der Mitte, der das Irgendwo der Standorte in eine neue, eine erste Ordnung hinüberrettet – 'Zone' bezeichnet sehr freiwillig das Schwanken des Planers zwischen Park und Platz, zwischen Landschaft und Stadt: Alternativen, die an diesem Ort gar keine sind; Fragen, die nach 20 Jahren leidvoller Hauptstadtplanung so nicht mehr gestellt werden sollten.

So wie hier Gegend, die halb zerstörte Villengegend, Ausgangspunkt der Planung sein muss, so kann das immer wieder Doppelte der Republik anstiften zu dem Versuch, beides zu tun – stadträumliche Definition und parkartige landschaftsbezogene Offenheit in *einer* Gestaltungsabsicht zu verankern: die erste und die zweite und die vielen heimlichen Hauptstädte der Republik, die Länder und der Bund, der Bundestag und der Bundesrat, Bonn und Bad Godesberg und eine Gegend dazwischen, Kapitänsvillen und Kanzlerkiste, kleinmütige Bescheidung und endlich erwachtes Repräsentationsbedürfnis – in dieser Bonner Zweiheit müsste sich das Öffentliche im Herzen dieser Republik entwickeln lassen – ein Feld, das Raum und Park zugleich ist, am ähnlichsten noch dem Campus angloamerikanischer Bildungsstätten, anpassungsfähig an die Art der ihn formulierenden Bauten und ihre Inhalte, solange sie denn 'öffentliche Sache' sind. Beharrend nur auf der räumlichen Dimension und Gestalt, die durch ihre Präzision das Heterogene, das bereits beliebig Vorhandene und das sich im nächsten Jahrzehnt dazu Entwickelnde in ein erkennbar Ganzes einbinden muss.

Dieser 200 x 200 m grosse Campus muss dabei vieles, fast alles leisten:
– die neue grüne Mitte sowieso;
– die zumindest optische Präsenz des Bundestags zur 'Stadt' an der Adenauerallee versucht er mit allen Mitteln: mit grossen, diagonalen Sichtschneisen, sozusagen so früh wie möglich, und gefiltert gegenüber dem Haus der Geschichte (die beiden Südländervertretungen sind natürlich arge Hindernisse; wer will wissen, wie lange noch);
– der Balance-Akt zwischen räumlicher Dichte des Campus-Innenraums und zusammenfassender Offenheit zum näheren Umfeld von Kanzleramt, Haus der Geschichte, neuem Pressezentrum an der Heussallee, Städtischem Kunstmuseum und natürlich dem Bundestag kann bei entsprechender Dimensionierung der Campusbauten mit Bravour geleistet werden;
– die fast barocke Tendenz des ringförmigen Bundestagsvorplatzes, als einziges herausgehoben, zentrales Element in das Campus-Geviert eingreifend, macht den Versuch, die viel zu niedrig geratene Eingangshalle hilfsweise aufzuwerten. Zu diesem Zweck könnte auch der Kunstgriff getan werden, das ohnehin von der B9 zum Rhein hin fallende Gelände in dieser Tendenz zu verstärken, um von der Campuskante ab mit einer Art Gegenhang hinauf zur Eingangshalle dem allzu Bescheidenen dieser Situation entgegenzuwirken.

'Zone' is the working title chosen by the author of the brief to suggest a search for a place in the centre to counteract the haphazard nature of the sites and create a new sense of order for the first time – 'zone' willingly reveals the planner's wavering between park and square, landscape and town: alternatives that are not alternatives on this site; questions that should not be put like this after 20 years of painstaking capital city planning.

An area like this half-destroyed villa district, has to be the starting point for the plan, and so the continuing schizophrenia of the Republic planted the notion of trying to do two things – anchoring definition in terms of urban space and creating park-like, landscape-related openness within *a single* design intention: the first and the second and the many secret capitals of the Republic, Länder and Federation, Bundestag and Bundesrat, Bonn and Bad Godesberg and the district in between, captains' villas and Chancellor's box, faint-hearted moderation and a desire for public prestige that has at last been awakened – the public element at the heart of this Republic would have to allow itself to develop in this Bonn duality – a field that is a space and a park at the same time, most similar to the campus in Anglo-American educational establishments, adaptable to the nature and contents of the buildings that formulate it, to the extent that they are a 'public matter'. All that can be insisted upon is spatial dimension and shape, which must use their precision to bind something heteregeneous into a recognizable whole, things that are already there and random and things that will develop in the next decade.

This 200 x 200 m campus must do most, indeed almost all of this:
– be a new green centre anyway
– attempt to give the Bundestag at least visual presence vis-à-vis the 'city' on Adenauerallee by all the means at its disposal: with large, diagonal visual breaks, as early as possible as it were, and filtered vis-à-vis the Haus der Geschichte (the two southern representatives' buildings are terrible obstacles of course; who claims to know for how much longer);
– a balancing act between the spatial density of the campus interior and the uniting openness towards the nearby context of Chancellor's Office, Haus der Geschichte, the new press centre in Heussallee, Städtisches Kunstmuseum and of course the Bundestag can be achieved with bravura if the campus buildings are of the correct dimensions;
– the almost baroque tendency of the circular space outside the Bundestag, biting into the campus square as the only stressed and central element, makes an attempt at enhancing the status of the entrance hall, which has turned out out be far too low. To this end the trick could also be played of strengthening to the tendency of the site to slope, anyway it drops from the main road down to the Rhine, and to create a kind of counter-slope from the edge of the campus to the entrance hall as a counter-effect to the all-too-modest quality of this situation.

Deutsches Rheuma-Forschungszentrum, Berlin

1988, Axel Schultes
in Bangert Jansen Scholz Schultes
mit Charlotte Frank

Wo ist das Pendant? fragte der Bauer – und kaufte das zweite Klavier: ein Pendant zu diesem Schwanstein mag entwerfen wer will – die Siemens-Villa hat ihren Partner von Anbeginn, den Garten und den Wannsee, die herrlichen Bäume, den Aussichtsturm, die Grotte, das Bootshaus ... Also kein Zweites, kein Gegenüber; am Ende würde die Loggia noch zur Symmetrieachse. Das Immanuel-Krankenhaus macht aber klar, wie es nicht geht: das horizontale Ausgreifen der neuen Baumassen hat den Ort bereits zur Gegend gemacht – die Teutsche Villa ist vertikal, bei aller Altbackenheit himmelwärts. Haben wir also auch gemacht: die Forschung zwei Geschosse in die Erde (kein Grundwasser ist zu bedenken), drei Normalgeschosse Rückwand für das alte Ensemble; die Dachlandschaft vermittelnd zwischen dem Gimignano der Loggia und dem Kyffhäuser der Villa. Zur Strasse eine weiche, kräftige Glasrundung – ein bisschen Zentrum darf das Rheuma-Zentrum wohl auch sein. Die vier Quadranten des Kleeblatts treffen sich mit ihren Diagonalen beim Kaffeetrinken – das zentrale Sockelgeschoss bringt die Häuser zum Funktionieren.

German Institute for Rheumatism Research, Berlin

1988, Axel Schultes
in Bangert Jansen Scholz Schultes
with Charlotte Frank

Where is the companion piece? asked the peasant – and bought the second piano: anyone is welcome to try to design a companion piece to this Oldschwanstein – the Siemens Villa has had its partners from the beginning, garden and Wannsee, magnificent trees, look-out tower, grotto, boathouse ... And so no second attempt, nothing set against it; though in the end the loggia would provide a symmetrical axis. The Immanuel Hospital shows how not to do it: the horizontal sprawl of the new buildings has already made the place into an area – the villa is vertical, strives heavenwards despite all its old-fashionedness. And so we did that too: research two storeys underground (no ground water problems), three normal storeys of back wall for the old buildings; the roofscape linking the Gimignano of the loggia with the Kyffhäuser of the villa. On the street side is a soft, powerful curve of glass – the Rheumatism Centre is probably allowed to be a bit of a centre. The diagonals of the four quadrants of the clover-leaf meet at coffee-time – the central base storey makes the buildings work.

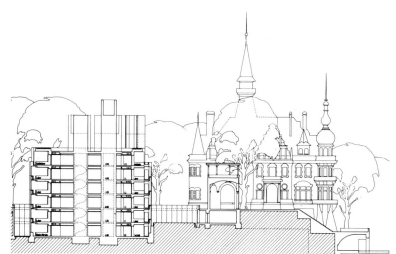

Grundriss 1. Untergeschoss
Grundriss Erdgeschoss

1st basement ground plan
ground floor ground plan

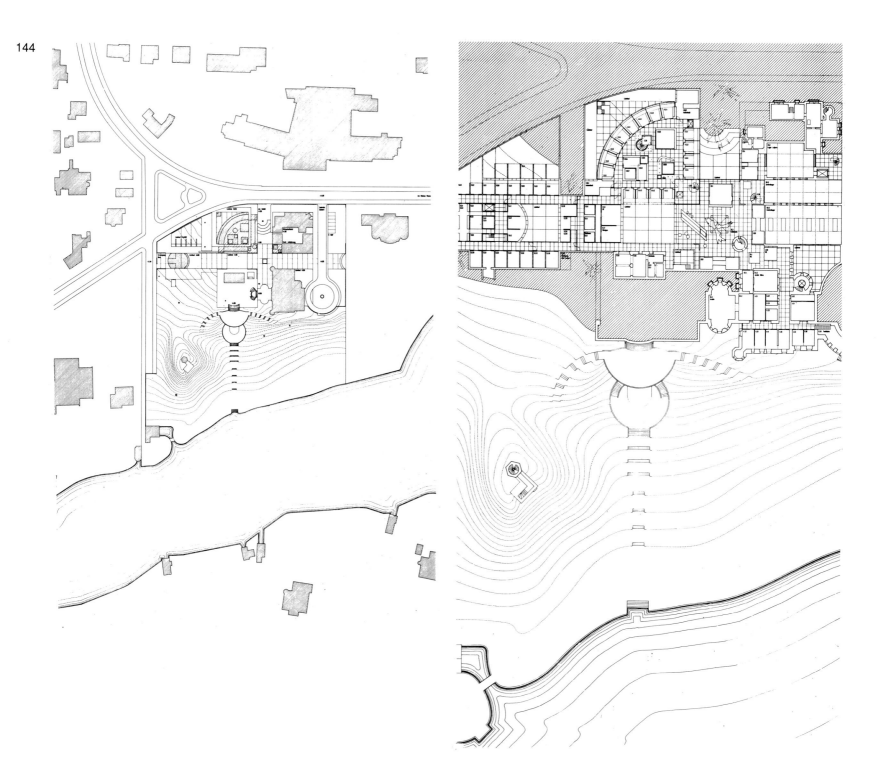

Grundriss 1. und 2. Obergeschoss

1st and 2nd floor ground plan

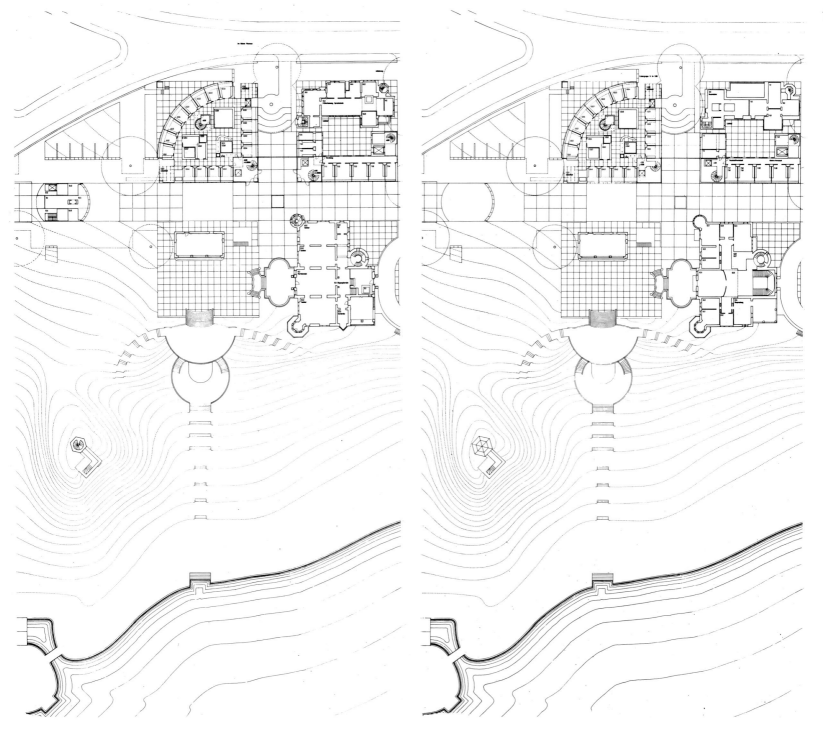

Schering AG offices, Berlin

1988, Axel Schultes, Stefan Scholz
in Bangert Jansen Scholz Schultes
with Charlotte Frank

How can we get Schering down to the Panke? If we want to give some perspective to the little river, now almost converted into a sewerage canal, and its possible green space, it needs a development concept to bring the imposing conglomerate of the two Schering blocks to a recognizable conclusion: the long, 36 m high wedge (no lower for this street 'profile', as long as humanly possible, close up to the transformer station) with the apparently inevitable bridges makes Sellerstrasse into Scheringstrasse and pursues its own ends with what is desirable in terms of urban development: orientating perhaps as many as 1,000 high-quality work places, protected from noise and exhaust gases, away from the road towards the south-east and the green space by the Panke, thus reaping a series of advantages:

– the Schering site's south-eastern flank, with its uproar of high-rise buildings behind it, has found both shape and a conclusion – no ridges, yards, compartments etc. etc. to make the place into an area. In terms of urban space the new building in Sellerstrasse deserves priority over building development in the depths of the plot. We in any case would feel that development of the edge of the block along Chausseestrasse would be extraordinarily harmful, particularly because of the legibility of the Schering area and the green space on the Panke: it would only be possible on a fragmentary basis anyway.

– the cross-section photographs – the building is anyway more of a cross section than a ground plan – show the essentials: the specialist rooms of the programme, the public element of the building, face the street – main entrance and approach of course, foyers and meeting rooms, conference and project rooms, cafés and toilets, galleries and steps – this demonstrates one of the points of the building, helps to paint the picture of the public face of Schering.

– the other element, the more private side of the building, is under the large glass slope, protected from the sun: the space in which the likes of us spend a large proportion of our lives, writing, telephoning: the office. This space was the design concept's central matter of concern: creating space, light and air in necessarily cramped conditions, with an individual room axis of 2.7 m. Model photographs 1:20 and 1:200 show that we have succeeded. Anyway the sample room that we created gave us a foolhardy hope: that it would be fun to work here.

Massenmodell, 1. Bauabschnitt
Massenmodell, 2. Bauabschnitt

full model, 1st building phase
full model, 2nd building phase

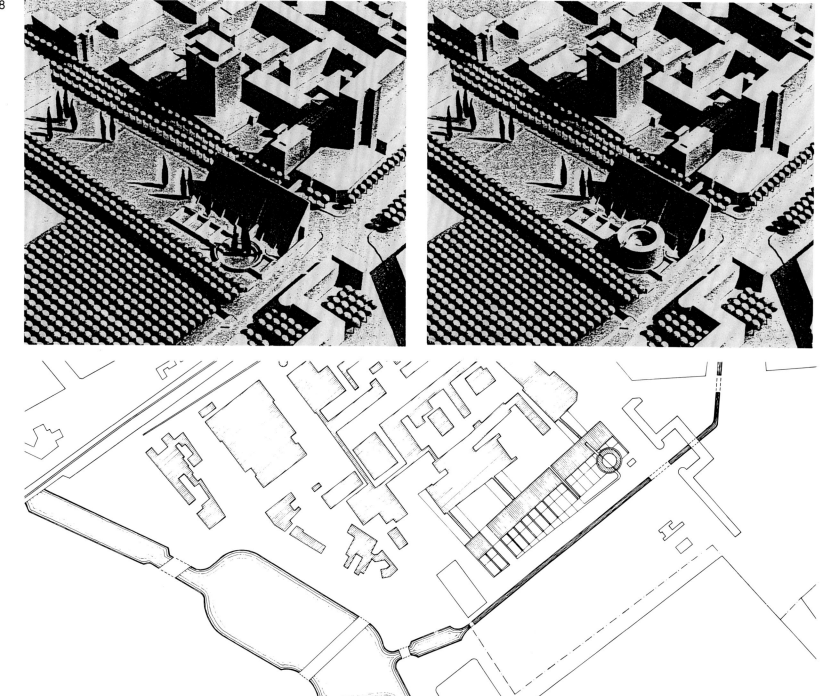

Massenmodell, 3. Bauabschnitt
Massenmodell, 4. Bauabschnitt

full model, 3rd building phase
full model, 4th building phase

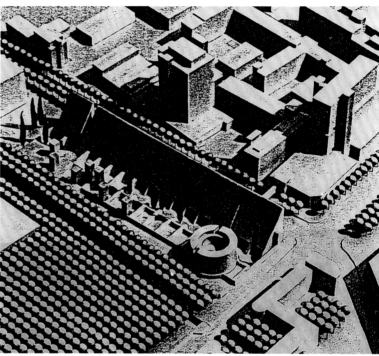
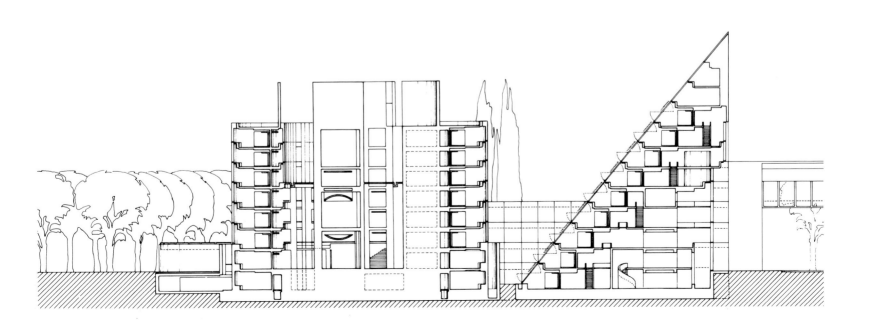

Grundriss Untergeschoss
Grundriss Erdgeschoss
Ansicht von der Panke

basement ground plan
ground floor ground plan
view from the Panke

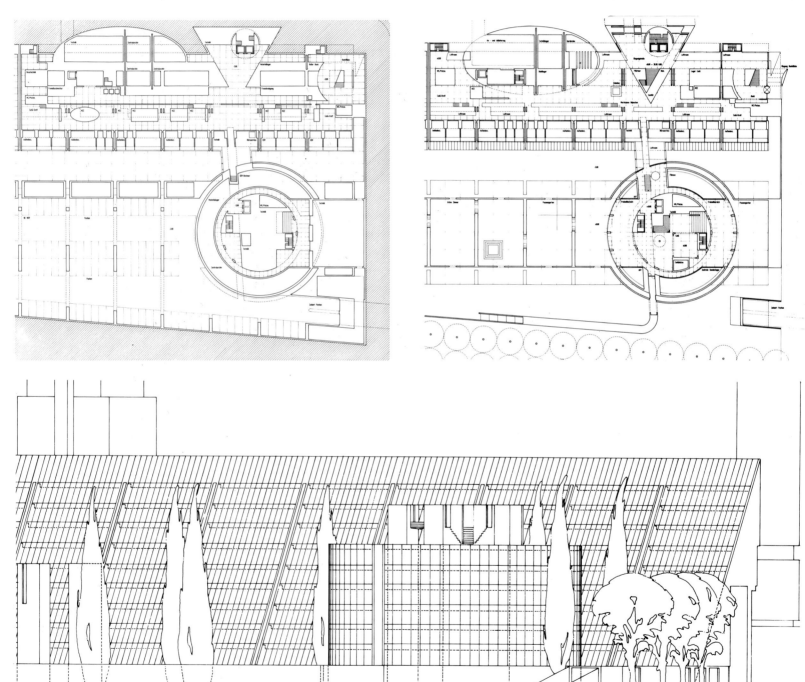

Grundriss 1. Obergeschoss
Grundriss 6. Obergeschoss
Ansicht von der Sellerstrasse

1st floor ground plan
6th floor ground plan
view from Sellerstrasse

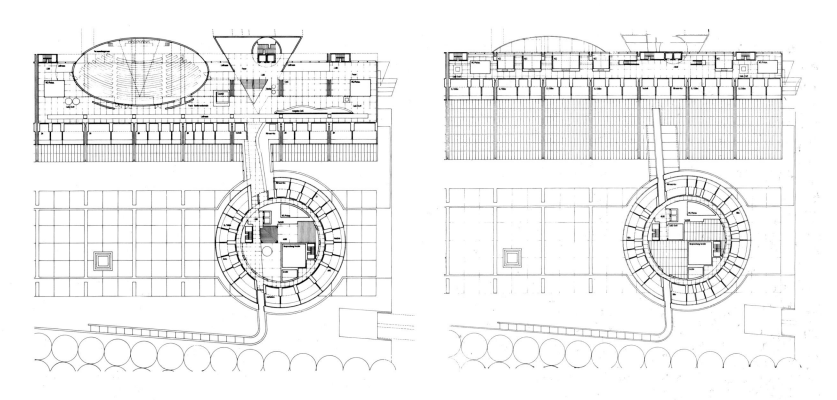

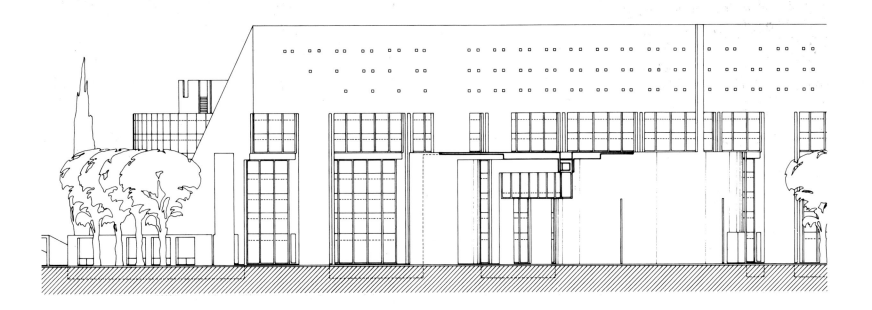

Schnittmodell · cross section model

Büro office

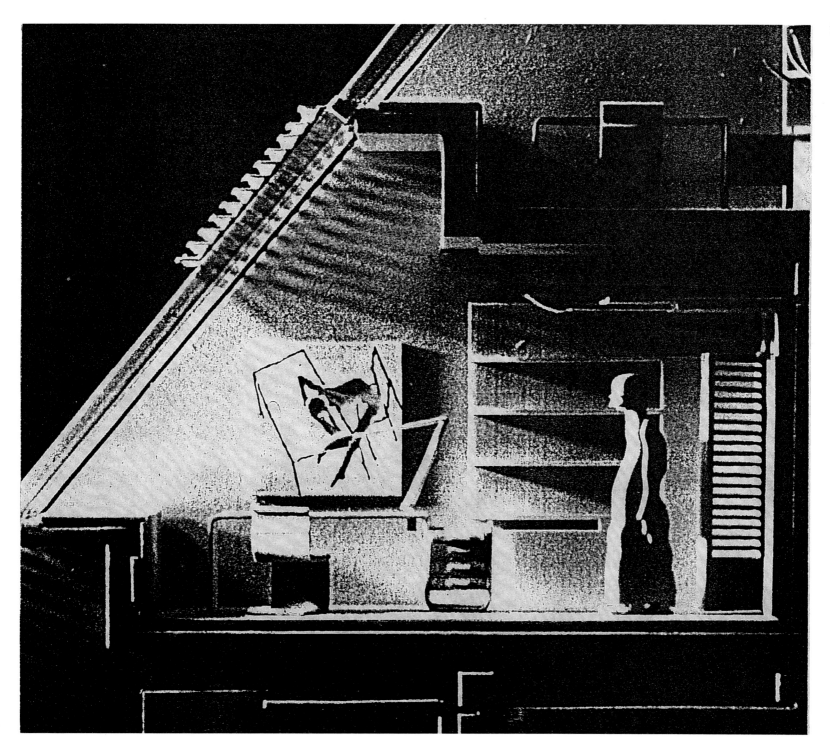

153

Deutsches Historisches Museum, Berlin

1988, Axel Schultes
in Bangert Jansen Scholz Schultes
mit Charlotte Frank, Georg Procakis

Wenn – wie in keinem anderen Museum – Zeit dargestellt werden muss, kann die Architektur gar nicht anders als ihren von Anbeginn durchgesiebten Herzenswunsch realisieren: den Käfig der drei Dimensionen in die vierte hinübermogeln – Zeit bauen. Hier wäre der Schlüssel, das Haus im Sinne der vom Museumsdirektor beschworenen 'geistigen Transparenz' der eigentlichen Bestimmung gegenüber aufzuschliessen. Dieser inwendigen Transparenz und Tiefe zuliebe sperrt sich das Haus nach draussen:

der *eine* Museumsraum mit seinen ringförmigen Terrassen ist offen nur in sich selbst und zum Himmel darüber, wie der ganze Bau eigentlich nur von der Wand als dem Königsmittel der Architektur Gebrauch macht – das Haus ist kein Kubus, seine Fassade ein einziges Fenster, das in den Himmel ... Wie anders als in der Abblendung des Draussen soll der Besucher die Konzentration aufbringen, die für ihn doch erst einmal verlorenen Zeiten wiederzufinden, wie anders als im Schutz des Zeitlosen: der Erde, des Wassers, der Sonne und der Wolken. Ein Schutz übrigens, der nicht zuletzt auch den alten Dingen, den Zeugen zusteht, den Exponaten. Das Museum lädt also auf eine eher stille Art ein – Pforte und Eingangshof vermitteln zwischen den zweitausend Jahren drinnen und dem Aufstand der Gegenwart draussen. Weniger die begrünten, baumgesäumten Wände dieses gebauten Stücks Tiergarten als die Turmkammern über den Spiegeldächern grüssen in die Berliner Runde. Das ausgeschlagene, grosse Vordach mit dem grosszügig verglasten Foyer darunter mag man also vermissen.

Die Aufgliederung der Ausstellungsfläche in eher antiquarische Darstellung von Geschichte auf der Seite der Epochenräume und in eine kritische Darstellung in Vertiefungs- und Themenräumen macht ein seit langer Zeit gehegtes räumliches Konzept zu einem Glücksfall: die wie Jahrhundertringe sich aufbauenden Epochenterrassen geben die Substanz für die sich aus ihnen heraus entwickelnden Themen- und Vertiefungstürme; der zyklisch gedachte Rundgang durch die Epochengalerien, der Weg von Heinrich dem Vogler auf einer Insel tief unter dem Berliner Sand bis hinauf aufs Dach mit dem Blick zum Alex und zum Potsdamer Platz macht die immer präsenten Themen- und Vertiefungsräume zum orientierungsstiftenden Mittelpunkt des Museums. Dieser Rhythmus von Weg und Ziel bestimmt zusammen mit der grossen Pause im Foyer die vielleicht drei bis fünf Stunden des Museumsbesuchs.

Die ringförmige Wechselausstellungshalle ist mit ihrer Raumhöhe äusserst grosszügig bemessen und transportiert damit Schmuggelware: auf fahrbaren Plattformen im 1. und 2. Obergeschoss kann wahlweise der Museums- und der Wechselausstellungsbereich ergänzt werden, bis hin zu der als Programmforderung fallengelassenen generellen Erweiterung. Unter Verzicht auf Tageslicht für die Wechselausstellung liesse sich das Museum um 8000 bis 10000 qm vergrössern. Auf das aktuelle Programm bezogen sollen die Plattformen flexibel da eingesetzt werden, wo die Ausstellungskonzeption Epochen- und Themenflächen über das feste Angebot des Museumskerns hinaus fordert.

Deutsches Historisches Museum, Berlin

1988, Axel Schultes
in Bangert Jansen Scholz Schultes
with Charlotte Frank, Georg Procakis

If, more than in any other museum, time is what has to be represented, then architecture can do no other than to realize its heart's desire, a desire with which it has been riddled from the beginning: to cheat the cage of three dimensions over into the fourth – to build time. This would be the key to opening up the building in the sense of the 'spiritual transparency' of its actual purpose, as conjured up by the director of the museum. For the sake of this inner transparency and depth the building is closed to the outside:

the *single* museum room with its circular terraces is open only to itself an to the sky above, as the whole building actually makes use only of the wall, the royal medium of architecture – the building is not a cube, its facade is a single window, a window into the sky ... how else than by blocking off the outside world is the visitor to find the concentration necessry to rediscover times that really are lost to him, how else than under the protection of the timeless: of earth, of water, of sun, of clouds. Protection, by the way, that is also due to the old things, the witnesses, the exhibits. The 'invitation to enter' issued by the museum is rather a silent one – gateway and entrance courtyard form a link between two thousand years inside and the rebellious present outside. A greeting to the cities of Berlin comes less from the planted, tree-lined walls of this built-up piece of the Tiergarten than from the tower chambers over the glazed, mirrored roof. You might therefore miss the large, protruding roof at the front with the generously glazed foyer underneath it.

Dividing the exhibiton space between essentially antiquarian presentation of history in epoch rooms, with critical presentation in consolidation and subject rooms, is a felicitous application of a long-cherished spatial concept: the epoch terraces, layered like centennial rings, provide substance for the subject and summary towers, which issue from them; the cyclical tour through the epoch galleries, a path leading from Henry the Fowler on a island depp below the Berlin sand up to the roof with its view of Alexanderplatz and Potsdamer Platz makes the omnipresent subject and summary towers into the nucleus of the museum – a permanent source of orientation. This rhythm of route and goal, together with the long pause in the foyer, gives shape to the three to five hour museum visit.

The circular gallery for temporary exhibitions is extremely generous in terms of height, which is used to house smuggled goods: mobile platforms on the first and second floors can be used to enlarge the museum or the temporary exhibition area, right up to the general extension, dropped as a programme demand. The museum could be enlarged by 8,000 to 10,000 sq m, but without daylight in the temporary exhibition area. As far as the present programme is concerned the platforms are to be used flexibly where the exhibiton plan requires epoch and subject areas beyond the fixed provision of the museum core.

Stadtraummodell, Spreebogen mit Reichstag und Kongresshalle
Grundriss 2. Untergeschoss
Grundriss 1. Untergeschoss

urban space model, Spree bend with Reichstag and Kongresshalle
2nd basement ground plan
1st basement ground plan

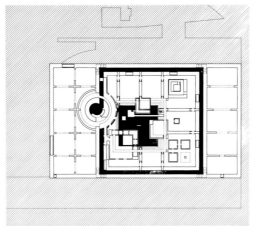
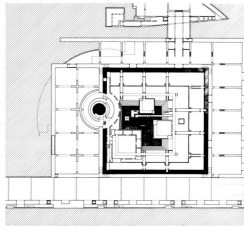

Massenmodell, Blick über Eingangshof nach Nord-Osten
Grundriss Erdgeschoss
Grundriss 1. Obergeschoss
Grundriss 2. Obergeschoss

full model, view north-east across entrance courtyard
ground floor ground plan
1st floorground plan
2nd floor ground plan

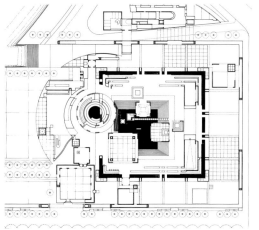
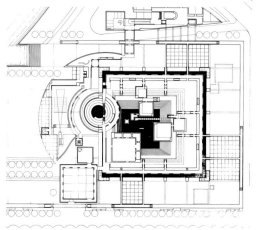
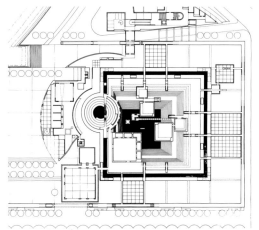

Grundriss 3. Obergeschoss   3rd floor ground plan

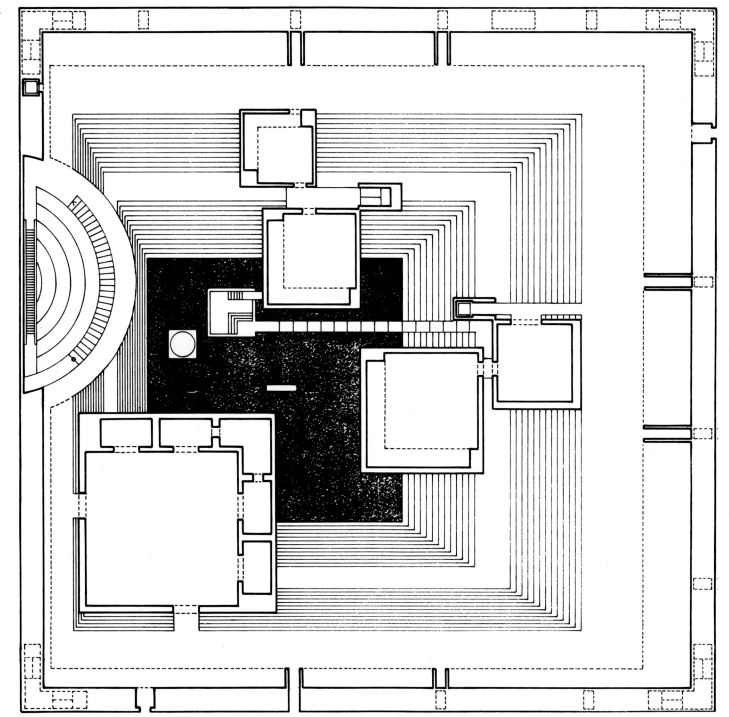

158

Schnittmodell   cross section model

Innenraummodell, Blick hoch ins Glasdach   interior model, view up into glass roof

Extension to Witten Town Hall

1987, Axel Schultes
in Bangert Jansen Scholz Schultes

The town hall extension is *the* opportunity for the town of Witten to make a decisive difference to the townscape with a single, relatively limited new building project: linked with building on the bus station site, the new town hall building will
– change the deserted square around bus area and garage ramp back into a sequence of streets and squares that makes sense to the citizens of the town,
– regulate the town's central crossroads (Hauptstrasse, Ruhrstrasse – Bahnhofstrasse, Johannisstrasse) in spatial terms and make it possible to experience them as street space and crossroads again,
– win back gestalt and significance for each of the subordinate urban spaces, by differentiated structuring of the spatially effective mass of the building;
 in brief, the new building on this most important site in the town can be the key to the development of a stimulating urban identity for the core of Witten – seen in terms of the inhospitableness of the present state of affairs a challenge to city council and planning authorities.

The extension building is conceived as a five-storey office-type structure following and continuing the adjacent town hall complex. The office wings with access by gallery in the suites in the old building are the formation that puts its stamp on the urban ground plan of the new town hall building. With their hundred double offices they are the administrative counterpart to the facilities offered by the special buildings, related to the public and also more political, assembled on the town hall terrace. These tower-like buildings opening in the diagonal to the pedestrian area contain as well as the new, second, main entrance the exhibition, the council chamber with gallery, two smaller conference rooms and the cafeteria with its roof terraces.

In the narrow space between the office galleries the grand staircase hall develops as the characteristic spatial element of the new building, creating orientation and transparency. At the steepest point of this six-storey interior, at the central lift nucleus, the grand staircase is as it were released into the spacious foyer areas of the exhibition and council chamber, and leads through the generously proportioned main entrance across to the town hall terrace, 2 metres above street level.

The roofscape of the tower buildings, sometimes almost peculiar in design, especially with the 'cloud' over the cafeteria terraces, is a reference to the local building tradition of the 50s, and also an attempt to establish optimism and good humour in the centre of Witten, as well as to use design as a way of minimizing initial fears of entering official buildings.

Dachaufsicht
Längsschnitt durch die Grosse Treppe

view of the rooftop
cross-section in longitudinal axis

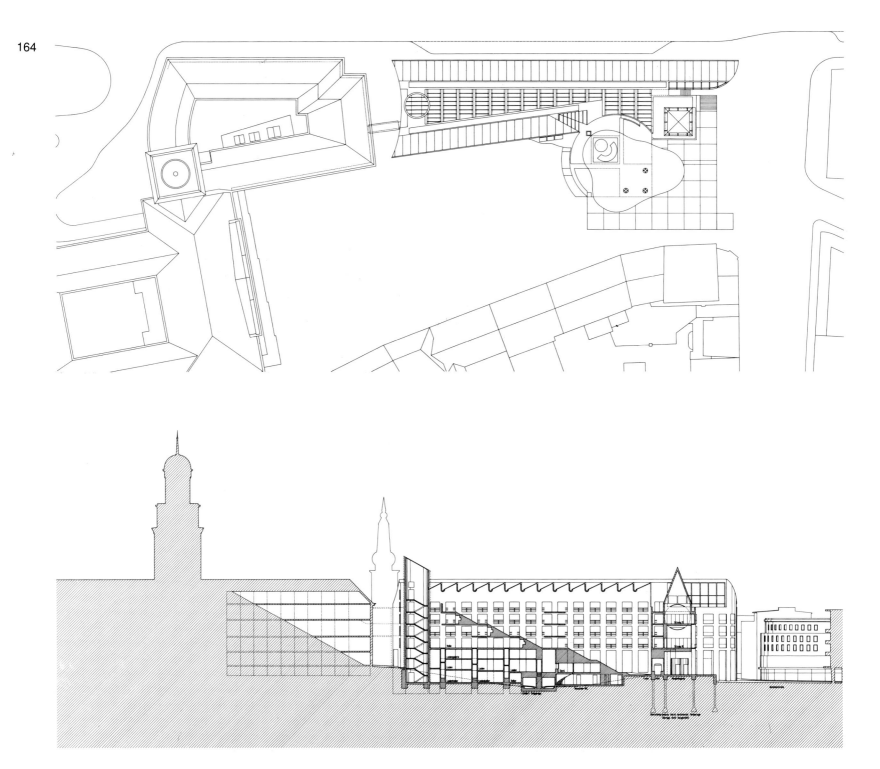

Grundriss Erdgeschoss
Grundriss 4.Obergeschoss

ground floor ground plan
4th floor ground plan

5 Lützowplatz, Berlin

1987, Bangert Jansen Scholz Schultes
with Jochen Gurt

The residential and business premises at 5 Lützowplatz form part of the eastern side of the square, 1–11 Lützowplatz, which is being rebuilt on the historic ground plan. The 60 m long north gable of 7 Lützowplatz with its extreme blinker effect and rooms in shade on the courtyard side makes building a twin or triplet with central access seem unsuitable. The plan is to build a maisonette-pergola bulkhead type of building, 19 m high and within the 12 m run of buildings of the whole new development, with housing for staircase and lift in the space between the new building and 7 Lützowplatz. The façade articulation will be two-storey in each case and relates to the scale of the old building façade with storey heights of over 5 m and would with the loggia and shop-window zone of the residential and commercial maisonettes turn the actual façade of the building towards the public space, which would also be a criticism of the square façade opposite.

Organization of living areas around central stairway and installation core is an attempt at various building stages to bridge the gulf between official ground plan standards and generous, spacious ideas for living.

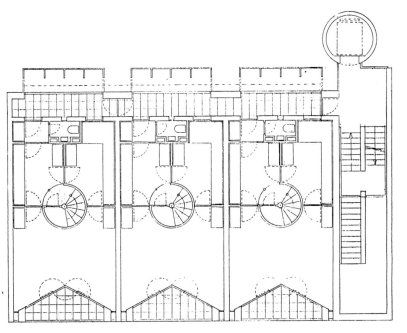
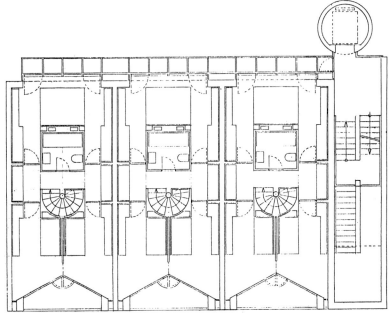

Museum für Völkerkunde, Frankfurt am Main

1986, Bangert Jansen Scholz Schultes

"Soldiers! Forty centuries look down upon you!" – this was Napoleon at the pyramids of Gizeh: how much longer from neolithic New Guinea to the civilization on Schaumainkai – here more than almost any where else architecture has to offer protection in its maternal function for the childlike and fragile products of the beginnings of culture; the distant, silent message declines into a collection of exotic curios in a late nineteenth century villa as much as in a product of international Post-Modernism, however instructive the discrepancy between it and our sweaty and sulphurous northern world may be.

And so it would be too good to be true to find architecture for this place that could insist radically enough on prefiguration to bridge this discrepancy, and make a home for even the most remote of objects; the Geometrical Convention, taken over into the metaphorical as regards content, was always in a position to do this, and this is how the concept for the ethnological museum in Frankfurt is to be understood:

the Petrified Forest, the Stone Tent, the Great Wall – all three pop up through the horizon of the park plane – totem, taboo and quite conventional craft work have to be reconciled.

Grundriss 2. Untergeschoss
Grundriss 1. Untergeschoss

2nd basement ground plan
1st basement ground plan

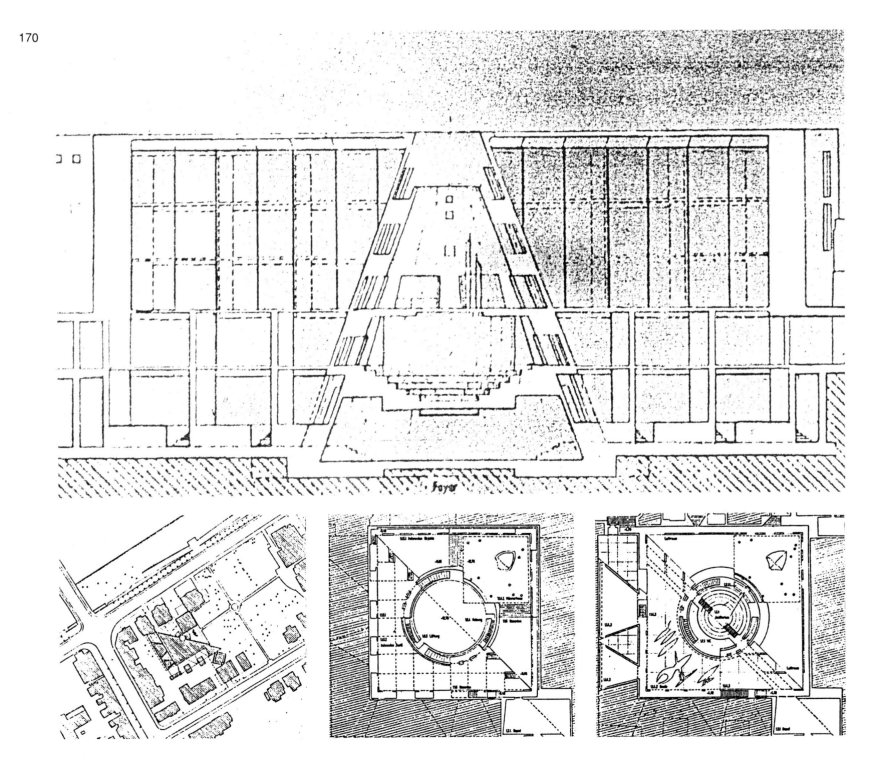

Grundriss Erdgeschoss
Grundriss 1. Obergeschoss
Grundriss 2. Obergeschoss

ground floor ground plan
1st floor ground plan
2nd floor ground plan

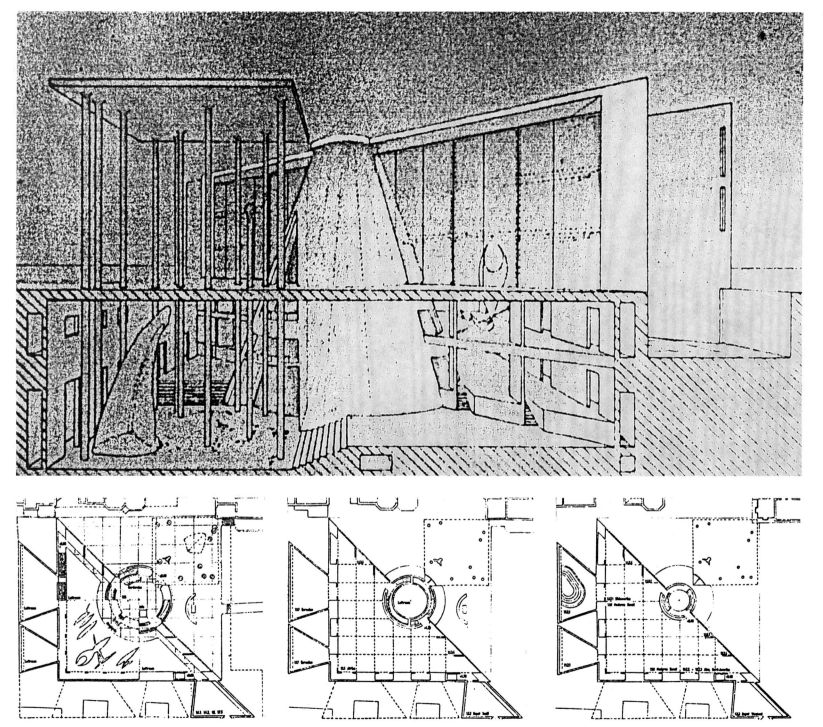

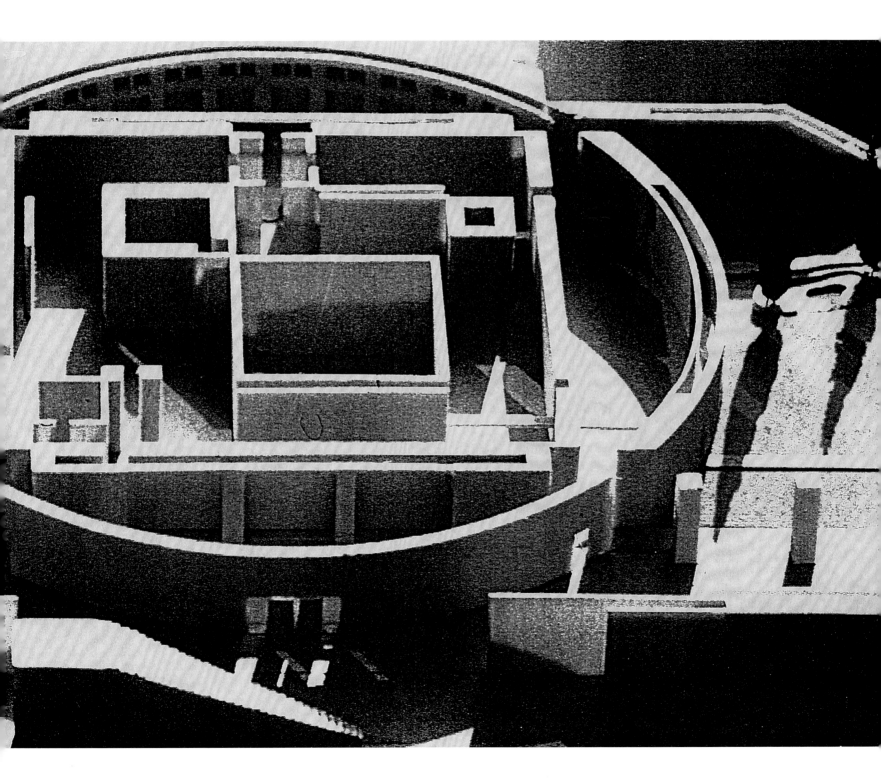

Kunst- und Ausstellungshalle Bonn

1986, Bangert Jansen Scholz Schultes
mit Hannelore Deubzer

Sicher wird noch viel Wasser den Rhein herunterfliessen, bevor sich die Bundesstrasse 9, die Friedrich-Ebert-Allee, zu den Champs-Elysées der Bundeshauptstadt gemausert hat – die Aneinanderreihung immer imposanterer Solitärbauten ohne diszipliniertes räumliches Konzept wird 'Stadt' in dieser Gegend jedenfalls eher verhindern. Dem Repräsentationsbedürfnis des Bundes lässt sich städtebaulich solider Rechnung tragen im Rahmen des Blockkonzeptes des 1. Preises des vorangegangenen Wettbewerbs:
zusammen mit dem Kunstmuseum auf dem damals als 'Museumsinsel' apostrophierten Bezirk ist die Bundeskunsthalle *der* Ort für Kunst- und Ausstellungsaktivitäten in der Bundeshauptstadt – die intensive baulich-räumliche Abstimmung zwischen den beiden Einrichtungen wird die eigentliche Attraktion des Standortes, den eigentlich beiderseitigen Nutzen und Vorteil ausmachen:
nicht die bauliche Inszenierung von Konkurrenz, sondern die optimale Entwicklung *eines* Ortes für Kunst auf einem selten so frei zu gestaltenden Gelände drängt sich hier auf. Eine andere Art von Inszenierung, nicht die postmodern gebrauchte des 'öffentlichen Raumes', ist hier gefordert: die Inszenierung, die Inszenierbarkeit der bildenden und darstellenden Künste, auch der nützlichen 'Künste', im neuen, grossen Haus der Kunsthalle.
In der Spannung zwischen dem instrumentellen, provisorischen Charakter einer Ausstellungsmaschinerie und der auf feste Räume, natürliches Licht und tiefes Material spekulierenden architektonischen Vorliebe versucht der Entwurf, wie denn anders, beides:
die zentrale Ausstellungshalle von 55 m im Quadrat bei 15 m lichter Höhe ist Werkzeug, Instrument in der Hand der Ausstellungsmacher; ihre raumkompositorischen Möglichkeiten sind Herausforderung an jede Ausstellungskonzeption, übrigens auch an die Ausstellungsmöglichkeiten anderswo. Die sich im üppigen Tageslicht präsentierende Halle ist in der vollen raumtechnischen Ausstattung (Hubböden, -wände, -lichtdecken) sicherlich auch eine Herausforderung an den Bauherrn – den finanziellen Aufwand hier schwerpunktmässig eher in die optimale Bespielbarkeit des Hauses als in repräsentative Überhöhung zu legen, kann für den Ruf und den Erfolg des Hauses von entscheidender Bedeutung sein.
Die ringförmige innere Foyer- und Ausstellungsfläche vermittelt zwischen der zentralen Halle und den unterschiedlichen inhaltlichen und funktionalen Randbedingungen des Umfeldes: Vorfahrt, Haupteingang, erstes Foyer und Café an der Friedrich-Ebert-Allee; Skulpturenterrasse und Skulpturensee zum Museum; Sonderausstellung, Bibliothek, Verwaltung und Parkplatzareal im Rückraum des Kunstviertels; Agora und südlicher Vorplatzbereich in direkter räumlicher Koppelung mit der Halle – dieses Foyer, der eigentlich dienende Raum im Gesamtgrundriss versucht keine Flexibilität, er beantwortet die an ihn gestellten, unterschiedlichsten Anforderungen in jeweils notwendiger architektonischer Ausformung: er muss Bühne sein können zwischen Halle und Agora; muss Entree machen mit Garderoben, Infos, WCs etc.; Ruhe- und Pausenzonen anbieten, z. B. am grossen Fenster zum See; zusätzliche Ausstellungsfläche anbieten, natürlich überall; nicht zuletzt aber auch neutraler Weg sein zu Einzelausstellungen, die sich in die grosse Halle teilen.

Kunst- und Ausstellungshalle Bonn

1986, Bangert Jansen Scholz Schultes
with Hannelore Deubzer

Certainly a great deal of water will flow down the Rhine before Bundesstrasse 9, Friedrich-Ebert-Allee, blossoms into the Champs-Elysées of the Federal capital – but in any case stringing together increasingly imposing individual buildings with no disciplined spatial concept will be more likely to hinder the emergence of 'city' in this district. The Federation's need to make an impression will be more solidly taken into account within the framework of the block plan put forward by the first-prize-winner of the preceding competition:
together with the Kunstmuseum, on what was for a time apostrophized as the 'museum island', the Kunsthalle is *the* place for art and exhibitions in the capital – intensive architectural and spatial co-ordination of the two institutions will be the actual attraction of the site, with actual advantages and gains for both:
what is essential here is not architectural stage-management of competing elements, but optimal development of *one* place for art on a site open to being shaped to a rare degree. It's not Post-Modernism's 'public space' that's needed here, but another kind of setting: staging and stageability of the fine and performing arts, and the useful 'arts', in the large, new Kunsthalle building.
Within the tension between the instrumental, provisional character of an exhibition machine and architectural preference speculating on fixed spaces, natural light and deep material, the design attempts – what other choice was open – to do both:
the central exhibition hall, 55 m square and 15 shining metres from floor to ceiling, is a tool, an instrument in the hands of the exhibition maker; its possibilities for composing of space are a challenge to any exhibition concept, and incidentally to exhibition possibilities elsewhere as well. The hall presents itself in abundant daylight, and its full spatial-technical equipment (mobile floors, walls, lighting gantries) certainly also makes it a challenge to the client – putting the thrust of financial effort in the optimum playability of the house rather than exorbitant prestigiousness can be of decisive importance for the reputation and success of this building.
The circular inner foyer and exhibition space forms a link between the central hall and the various functional and technical fringe elements in the surrounding area: approach, main entrance, first foyer and café in Friedrich-Ebert-Allee; sculpture terrace and sculpture lake on the museum side; special exhibition, library, administration and parking area in the space behind the art quarter; agora and south square in front of the building in direct spatial contact with the hall – this foyer, the actual working room in the overall ground plan, makes no attempt at flexibility, it responds to the various demands made upon it with the architectural shape appropriate in each case: it must be able to form a stage between hall and agora; must be an entrance space with cloakrooms, toilets etc.; offer rest and break spaces, by the big window overlooking the lake, for example; offer additional exhibition space, not everywhere, of course; but not least also be a neutral route to individual exhibitions sharing the large hall.

174

Friedrich - Ebert - Allee

Massenmodell, Wettbewerb Kunstmuseum
Massenmodell, Wettbewerb Kunsthalle

full model, Kunstmuseum competition
full model, Kunsthalle competition

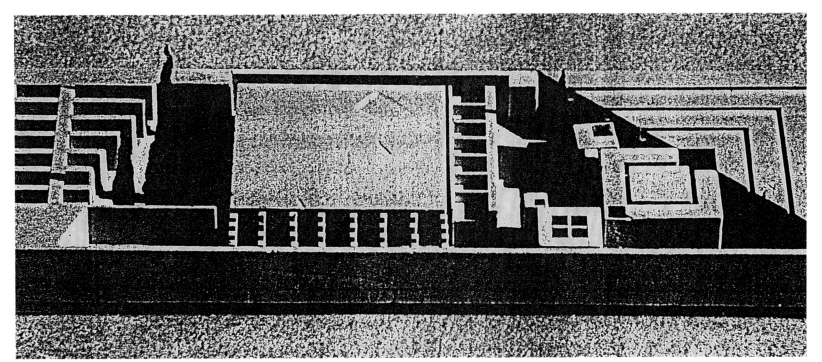

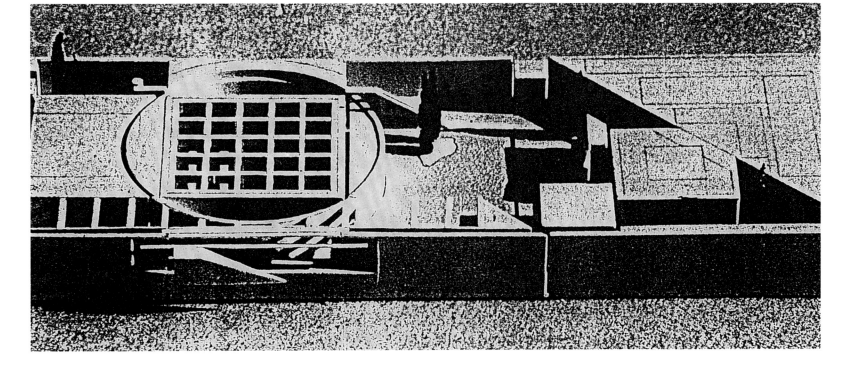

Länge läuft, Variationen über eine Ausstellung	length runs, variations on an exhibition
immer an der Wand lang	always along the wall
ein Filmfestspiel – Häuser und Plätze	a film festival – buildings and squares
Centre Court – Africa	Centre Court – Africa
gross und klein	large and small
Karneval in Bonn	carnival in Bonn

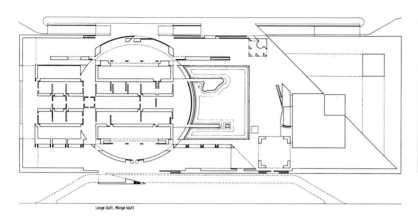

Länge läuft, Mänge käuft

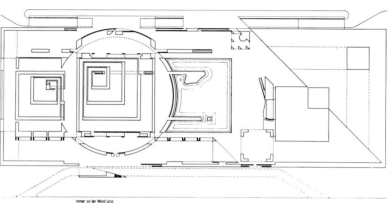

immer an der Wand lang

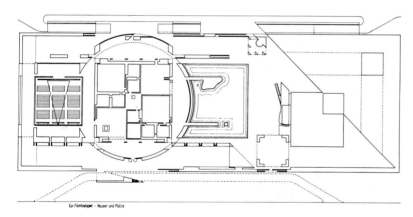

Ein Filmfestspiel – Häuser und Plätze

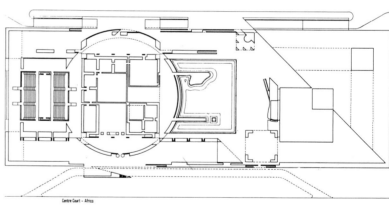

Centre Court – Africa

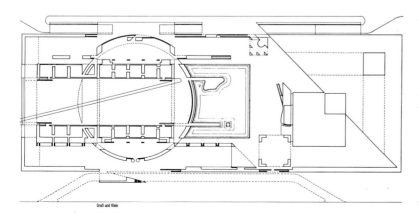

Groß und Klein

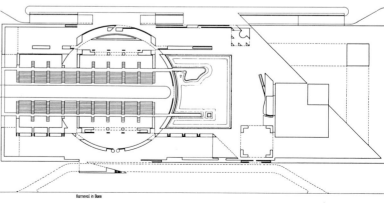

Karneval in Bonn

Ariadne – vier Maler
Schätze aus der verbotenen Stadt
bei uns zuhause in Italien – Hommage an T.
die grosse Retroperspektive
3000 Plätze
Rheingold

Ariadne – four painters
treasures from the forbidden city
at home in Italy – homage to T
the great retroperspective
3,000 seats
Rheingold

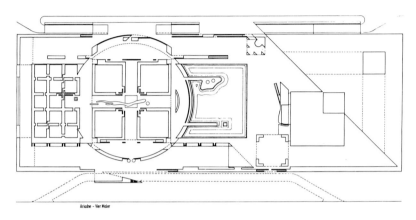

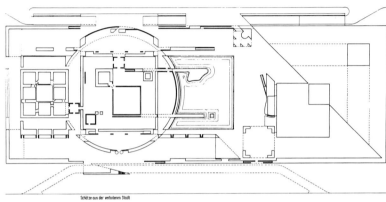

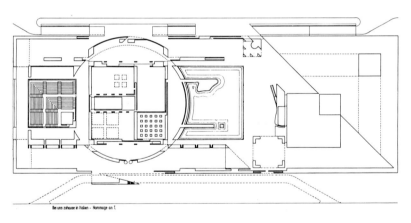

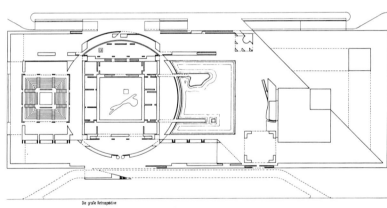

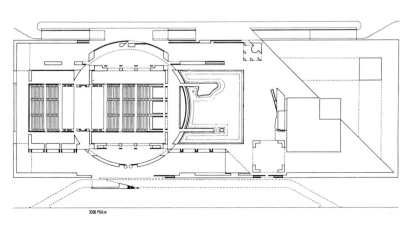

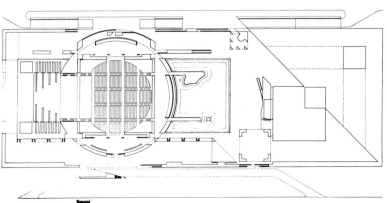

die grosse Retroperspektive
3000 Plätze

the great retroperspective
3,000 seats

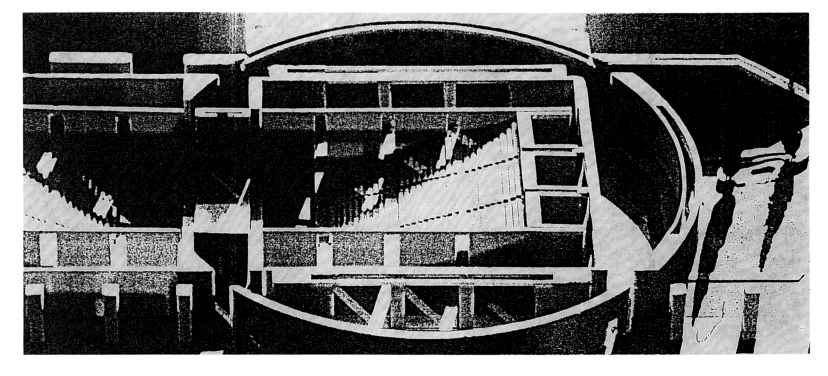

vier Maler
Rheingold

four painters
Rheingold

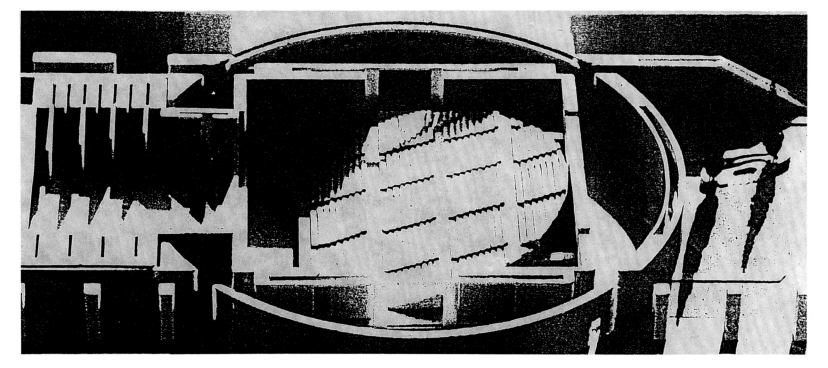

Städtisches Kunstmuseum Bonn

1985, Axel Schultes
in Bangert Jansen Scholz Schultes
with Jürgen Pleuser

No Place, Nowhere – somewhere between Bonn and Godesberg a claim has to be staked for art – 100 by 300 metres – that could be a small town – why not? – there isn't one here already. Garnishing the area with a few art temples – that will certainly be attempted, but how do you occupy a place that isn't?

A town is to be created along Friedrich-Ebert-Allee – in the west with museums as closing edge of the space, as high as Bonn once was: 15 m; to the east down to the Rhine a loose sequence of monuments, not monuments as yet, freely placed in a park landscape.

A museum too is only a building, it doesn't have to conform to a particular type, but: there are some typical features: here for example top light everywhere – the Villa Imperiale in Tivoli, here in the Bonn city precincts with the block edge all around – isn't that already it? The old wharf in Barcelona, cut open diagonally like Le Corbusuier's 'endless' museum, halved; the great mosque in Cordoba, although you'd have to do without the orange grove; all these are magnificent museums if only the light is right, and the running metres of wall – rooms with individuality *and* common sense, precisely for the one artist and the far too many ... the suggestion may be seen thus or similarly:
– the large wall on which you can walk on the Allee side gives status in terms of urban space, designates place, is a foil for open-air sculpture; wide open to the Heussallee junction for example or completely walled in except for the approach portal to screen the internal spaces, the table a focus for the sculpture courts;
– the central hall of the foyer and the temporary exhibition dominates the three diagonal paths through the sculpture courts and thus frees the space for the opening of the four exhibition aisles into the squares;
– the Kunsthalle is linked to the approach and the Allee space through the glass-roofed columns by the wall, perforated here as an open foyer, but orientates itself with equal weight with the loggia running the whole length of the building to the core of the square and courtyard spaces between the table and the rear entrance;
– the spare buildings cited as mere ciphers could be used for example as a residential and studio facility for guest artists, symposia, workshops and things of this kind.

If Thomas Mann's remark: 'art must become recognition' could almost be a motto for the new museum, particularly in relation to contemporary art, this saying is also particularly true for the contents architectural language must communicate – highly contradictory contents in any case:

in the tension between a town's political need for prestige and the necessities of urban planning – of public-general putting-on-show and personal and private experience of art, the architectural concept would have to achieve almost the impossible, amidst Post-Modern clatterings: it would have to allow convention to stand in such a way, to rescue it for the new in such a way, that handling form and space, an individual matter anyway, could become the starting point for a new compulsoriness – this is a move towards the classical, just as a balance must be struck, the balance of monumental and comfortable, droll and banal, coarse and fine, solid and filigree, the living development of the building.

182

Max Ernst
Grundriss Erdgeschoss
Grundriss 1. Obergeschoss

Max Ernst
ground floor ground plan
first floor ground plan

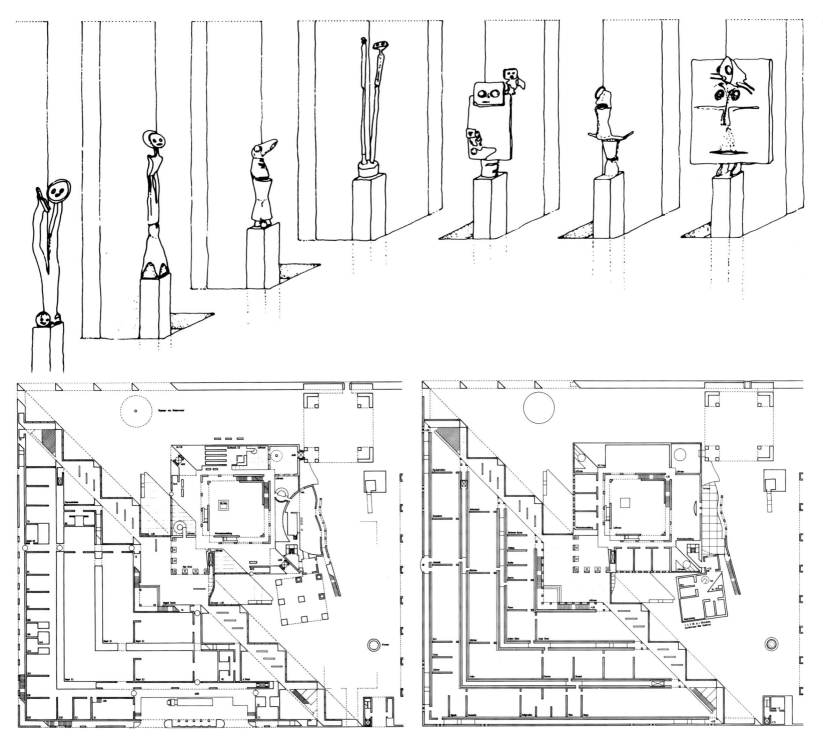

Schnittmodell – Wechselausstellung, Foyer, Hörsaal cross-section model – temporary exhibition, foyer, auditorium

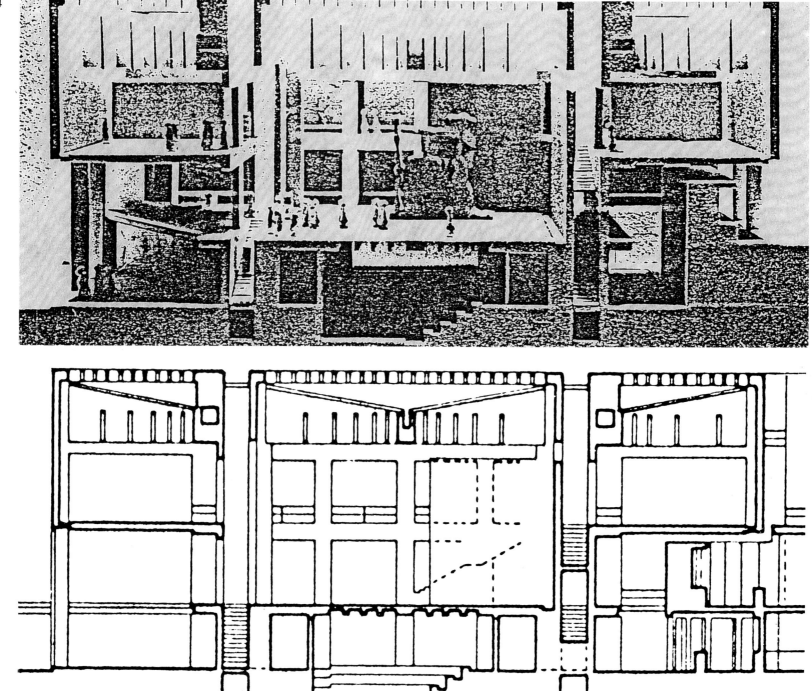

Schnittmodell – Sammlung, Depots   cross-section model – collection, storerooms

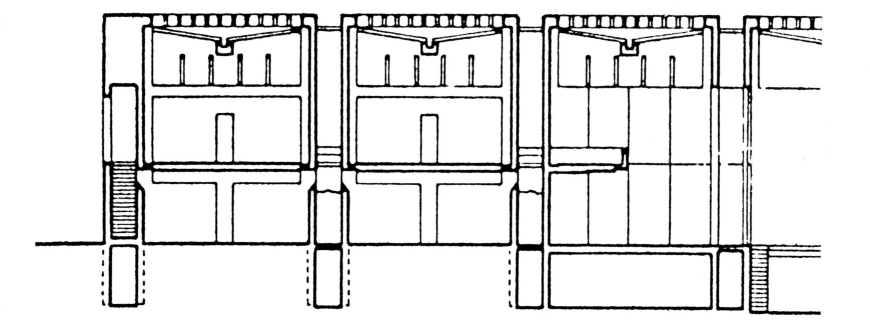

Massenmodell – die offene Ecke · full model – the open corner

186

Massenmodell – Verwaltung, Café, Loggia   full model – administration, café, loggia

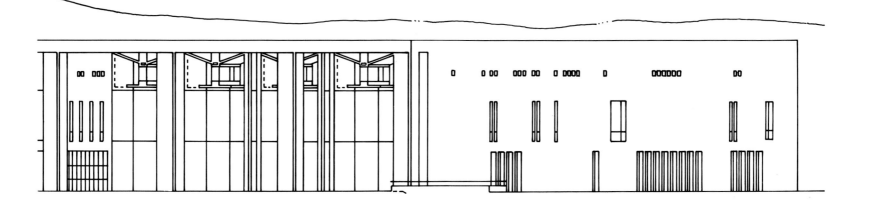

Hängepartie

'... kein Buch: was liegt an Büchern!' – kein Œuvre-Anlauf, eher schon eine Kontrolle auf's Eigene hin, auf die Methode, auf die Einübung in Architektur – ein kritischer Blick sozusagen auf den Proviant: ob's denn reicht und lohnt für den Rest der Reise.

Die Schubladen des Architekten als Fundbüro: 'seit ich des Suchens müde ward, verlegt' ich mich aufs Finden', seitdem das Beste einer Produktion, einer Wettbewerbsproduktion, einer leicht vergänglichen also vor allem, auf Halde geschoben wird, werd' ich nicht anders als den so aufgetürmten, sich verdichtenden Fundus, wie Dr. Murkes gesammeltes Schweigen, für neue Erfahrungen ausbeuten – ein gefährlich kurzschlüssiges Recycling allemal, wenn die Probe aufs Exempel zu selten oder nur, wie beim Bonner Museum, am deformierten Objekt gemacht werden kann.

Das Bündel von Arbeiten der letzten sieben Jahre hilft mir dabei auf die Sprünge – von heute nach gestern, wie im Aktenordner: Sucht und Suche nach suggestiver Räumlichkeit, einer sehr unzeitgemässen Sucht offensichtlich. Dabei ist es bei der erstbesten Architekturveranstaltung mit Händen zu greifen, im neubabylonischen Aneinandervorbeihören der Kollegen: was unseren nachmodernen Pluralismus bei aller Buntheit so belanglos macht, ist das Fehlen einer Hierarchie in der planerischen Qualität, das Fehlen eines Masstabs, ein Mangel an Instinkt für das Wesentliche. Das mal aufgeregte, mal müde Verhältnis zur Architektur, das antiquarische Spiel mit Typen und Formen, den alten und den eigenen, die bequeme, auch mal virtuose Beschäftigung mit den Mitteln statt mit den Zielen von Architektur ist das Ergebnis dieser Desorientierung.

Was not tut, um diesem Uneigentlichen in der Architektur beizukommen, nach 400 Jahren Postrenaissance und der Hoffnung der Moderne, ist eine Morphologie, eine Dramaturgie des Raumes, die das Streben nach Gestalt auf die Entwicklung neuer Räume und Raumtypen wendet – mit der verwegenen Hoffnung, eine neue, uralte Konvention, einen architektonischen Imperativ herauszubilden.

'Alles ist Raum', sagen die Modernsten – und machen damit unsere Kunst zum Kunstgewerbe. 'Schönes in dieser schönen Arbeit' ist nur zu leisten in der präzisen Abgrenzung von Raum durch die Schwere des Materials und beseelt durch das Licht. Einer solchen Raumpflege möchte ich mit dieser Materialsammlung – gerade bei den Jüngeren – Platz schaffen.

a.s.

eine Studienarbeit, 1966

Game adjourned

'... not a book, what's important about books!' – not an attempt to define an œuvre, but more a check on my own work, on my methods, my practice as an architect – a critical look, as it were, at the stores: whether there's enough for the rest of the journey, whether it's worth while.

The architect's drawer as lost property office: 'I got tired of looking so changed to finding', since the best things produced, produced for competitions, so particularly prone to transitoriness, are pushed away into a heap, I intend to use this dense pile of material, like the sound editor who collected silence, as something to exploit for new experiences – rash and dangerous recycling in every case: proof is all too rarely concrete, or only present, as is the case with the Bonn museum, as a distorted object.

This bundle of work over the last seven years gives me a helping hand – from today to yesterday, as in a file: obsession with and search for suggestive spatiality, apparently a most untimely obsession. But it's absolutely obvious at any old architectural event, from the neo-Babylonian way colleagues fail to listen to each other: what makes our Post-Modern pluralism so trivial despite all its colourfulness is lack of a hierarchy of planning quality, lack of scale, lack of instinct for the essential. And the result of this disorientation is a relationship with architecture that is sometimes excited, sometimes weary, an antiquarian game with types and forms, old ones and one' own, a comfortable and sometimes virtuoso concern with architectural meansnot architectural ends.

What is needed to deal with this impropriety in architecture after 400 years of post-Renaissance and the hopes of Modernism, is a morphology, a dramaturgy of space: this will turn striving after gestalt towards the development of new spaces and spatial types – in the foolhardy hope that a new, age-old convention, an architectural imperative can be formed from this.

'Everything is space' say the most modern – and thus make our art into a circus. 'Beauty in this beautiful work' can only be achieved by precise delineation of space by weight of material, inspired by light. I should like this collection of material to make room for such caring treatment of space, at least, above all, for younger people.

a.s.

student work, 1966

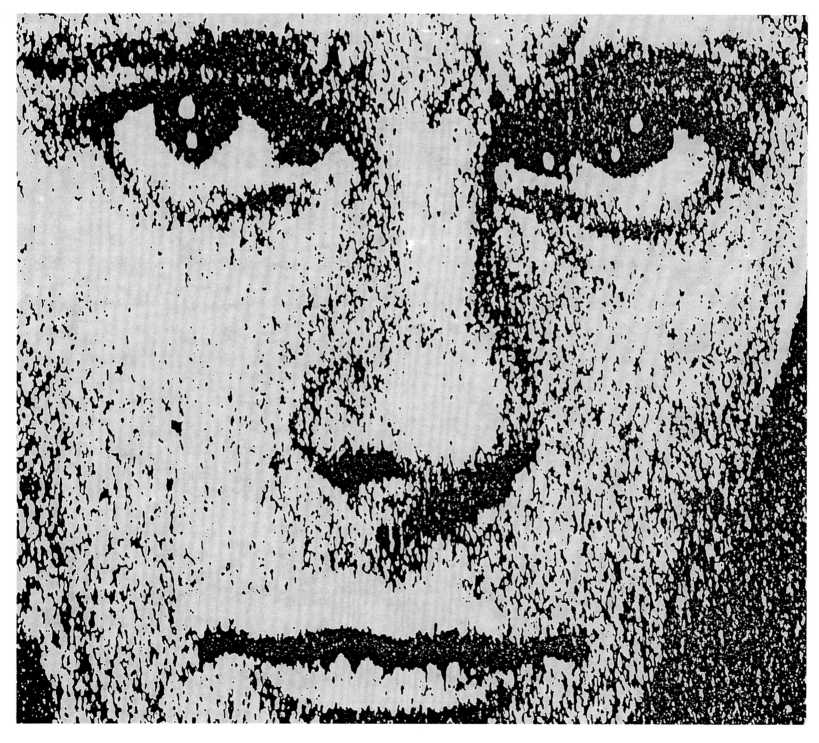

Vita

*17.11.1943	Dresden	... komme, und weiss nicht woher
1963–1969	TU Berlin	... bin, und weiss nicht wer,
1969–1991	BJSS	... gehe, und weiss nicht, wohin,
1992–		... mich wundert, dass ich so fröhlich bin.

Mitarbeiter

Collaboraters

Potsdamer Bahnhof, Berlin: Charlotte Frank

Potsdamer Platz, Berlin: Charlotte Frank Marika Lemper, Andreas Voigt, Daniela Andresen, Stefan Eich, Stefan Reik, Christian Franke, Stephan Ernst

Gewerbepark Gladbeck-Brauck: Charlotte Frank Marika Lemper, Klaus Gayer, Stefan Eich, Georg van Beers

Deutsche Bank Unter den Linden, Berlin: Charlotte Frank, Christoph Witt Daniela Andresen, Margret Kister, Christian Franke, Thomas Meyer

Bürozentrum Hemmerichsweg, Frankfurt: Charlotte Frank Marika Lemper, Erich Gassmann, Thomas Meyer, Ulrich Kellersmann, Stefan Reik, Stefan Eich

Berlin Friedrichstadt: Charlotte Frank Erich Gassmann, Michael Bürger, Daniela Andresen, Volker Staab, Marika Lemper, Margarete Stephan, Klaus Neumann, Heike Büttner, Brigitta Weise, Stephan Ernst, Thomas Meyer, Christian Franke

Altmarkt Dresden: Charlotte Frank Daniela Andresen, Michael Bürger, Klaus Gayer, Alfred Nieuvenhuizen, Christian Franke, Erich Gassmann

Piazzale Roma, Venedig: Charlotte Frank Daniela Andresen, Michael Bürger, Margret Kister, Christian Franke, Thomas Meyer, Stephan Ernst, Sipke Kingma

Rathauserweiterung Witten: Charlotte Frank, Joachim Koob, Daniela Andresen, Erk Meinertz

Expo '92 Sevilla: Charlotte Frank, Joachim Koob Detlef Junkers

Dachaufbau Lützowplatz 7, Berlin: Charlotte Frank Michael Bürger

Haus der Geschichte, Stuttgart: Charlotte Frank Joachim Koob Daniela Andresen, Detlef Junkers

Wohnen an der Hasenheide, Berlin : Charlotte Frank, Joachim Koob Angela Schmidtutz

Büropark am Welfenplatz, Hannover: Charlotte Frank Daniela Andresen, Andreas Voigt, Joachim Koob

Haus am Michel, Hamburg: Charlotte Frank Joachim Koob Angela Schmidtutz, Claudia Liss

Tokyo International Forum: Charlotte Frank, Joachim Koob

Internationaler Seegerichtshof, Hamburg: Charlotte Frank Joachim Koob Claudia Liss, Stefan Eich, Thomas Krasenbrink, Stephan Ernst

Bibliotheca Alexandrina: Charlotte Frank Joachim Koob, Andreas Voigt, Angela Schmidtutz, Thomas Krasenbrink, Stephan Ernst, Konrad Benstz, Arndt Kerber

Berlin Museum: Charlotte Frank Volker Staab, Thomas Krasenbrink Angela Schmidtutz, Petra Cordes

Dachaufbau Lützowplatz 7, Berlin: Charlotte Frank Joachim Koob

Familiengericht, Berlin: Charlotte Frank Joachim Koob Stephan Ernst, Andreas Voigt

Intercity-Hotel, Berlin: Charlotte Frank Joachim Koob Petra Cordes, Christian Bechtle, Heike Nordmann

Parlamentsvorzone Bonn: Charlotte Frank, Joachim Koob, Jürgen Pleuser

Deutsches Rheuma-Forschungszentrum, Berlin: Charlotte Frank Gerd Münster Christian Bechtle, Joachim Koob, Georg Procakis, Stephan Ernst, Michael Bürger

Schering AG, Berlin: Charlotte Frank Gerd Münster, Volker Staab, Michael Bürger Joachim Koob, Stephan Ernst, Christian Bechtle, Georg Bumiller, Georg Procakis

Deutsches Historisches Museum, Berlin: Charlotte Frank, Georg Procakis Ingrid Amann, Michael Bürger, Rebecca Chestnutt, Hannelore Deubzer, Volker Staab, Joachim Koob, Tibor Karsai, Stephan Ernst

Rathauserweiterung Witten: Charlotte Frank, Carla Vallotto, Sue Weigelt, Stephan Ernst, Tibor Karsai, Andreas Voigt

Lützowplatz 5, Berlin: Jochen Gurt Andreas Voigt, Maude Kohlhardt, Andreas Wolf

Museum für Völkerkunde, Frankfurt: Georg Bumiller, Enno Maass, Andreas Voigt Rebecca Chestnutt, Georg Meissner, Danielle Vergeres

Kunst- und Ausstellungshalle Bonn: Hannelore Deubzer Peter Bendoraitis, Jochen Gurt, Georg Meissner, Verena von Beckenrath

Kunstmuseum Bonn: Jürgen Pleuser Rebecca Chestnutt, Georg Meissner, Peter Bendoraitis, Christoph Witt, Bernd Reinecke, Josefa Seppeler, Michael Schaedler, Hannelore Deubzer

vor der Bonner Baustelle, 1990

- die zentrale Treppe
- vom Foyer hoch zur Ausstellung
- von der zentralen Treppe zur Wechselausstellung
- von der zentralen Treppe zur Wechselausstellung
- ein Raum der Wechselausstellung
- das Oberlicht
- die Ausstellung
- Licht
- unter dem Hauptzugang

in front of the Bonn building site, 1990

- the central stairs
- from the foyer up to the exhibition
- from the central stairs to the temporary exhibition
- from the central stairs to the temporary exhibition
- a room in the temporary exhibition
- the skylight
- the exhibition
- light
- under the principal access